CANAL CRIMES

CANAL CRIMES

R. H. DAVIES

AMBERLEY

First published 2010

Amberley Publishing
Cirencester Road, Chalford,
Stroud, Gloucestershire, GL6 8PE

www.amberleybooks.com

British Library Cataloguing in Publication Data.
A catalogue record for this book is available from the British Library.

ISBN 978 1 4456 0045 1

Typesetting and Origination by FONTHILLDESIGN.
Printed in Great Britain.

Contents

My thanks go to several persons and institutions without whose help this publication would have been impossible: the staff at the William Salt Library in Stafford, who allowed me to see the original copies of *The Stafford Advertiser*, which contain the accounts of the Christina Collins trials reproduced in chapters 6 and 8; Stafford Library; the Black Country Society, who do such good work and have allowed me to use the account of Elwell *v.* the BCN from their excellent magazine; Rob Taylor at the *Black Country Bugle* for the Jane Doley piece; Wolverhampton Archives; the *Waterways World* team; Alan Faulkner for superb images; Lee Jackson for the same; I have used cases from the Old Bailey courtesy of the Old Bailey Online project and a few quotes from the new online source of information – Wikipedia; Richard Clark, who has done some fine work regarding crime and capital punishment; to Campbell McCutcheon for excellent illustrations regarding the Old Bailey and Newgate; to Nicola Gale for refining the manuscript and getting rid of my errors.

CHAPTER 1

Crime on the Waterways

Many forms of crime, and punishments for those crimes, have been with us throughout the history of mankind. The nineteenth and early twentieth centuries – or as I shall loosely term it here, the age of the industrial canal – were no exception. Burke and Hare, possibly two of the earliest and most famous serial killers from Scotland in the 1820s, did not commit their murders by the canal, but interestingly, both had worked as navvies on the New Union Canal. Whilst lodging in Edinburgh, the pair discovered that good money could be had by supplying 'fresh' corpses to the dissection schools. Poverty may have been behind some of the crimes featured in this book, but criminologists will argue that some criminals steal even when they have plenty, so motivation for crime has always been an interesting subject to ponder. Trawling through cases from the Old Bailey and Stafford County Assizes, one quickly realises that all forms of crime visited

Regent's Canal: City Basin. (A. Faulkner)

Horse boat at work, twentieth century. (D. Wilson)

the waterways of Britain. In this publication, we will look at several forms, from simple pickpocketing, through to drunkenness, violent robbery, child cruelty, prostitution, rape, manslaughter, murder, and even a feud over water rights. This was between a prominent Midland iron master and the Birmingham Canal Navigations Company. That hotly disputed and expensive case rumbled along for some seventeen years.

The crimes cover an area from Liverpool to London, but of more interest are the felons and the witnesses who are drawn from their ordinary lives into the solemnity of the courtroom. As for format, I have, for most cases, set them down as though one were in the court with them, listening to the legal teams as they question and cross-examine the perpetrators and witnesses. These fascinating folk, including wharfingers and company clerks, appear just like players in a drama, running the social spectrum from surgeons and policemen, to pub landlords, and of course, in case we forget, the humble boatman and his wife. From these authentic transcripts, we hear their real voices, echoing down through the decades, which adds to the realism and flavour of the court scenes.

The murder of Christina Collins on the Trent & Mersey Canal is a typical example of this treatment. Oh yes, that case has certainly been covered in other publications, but always as a shortened narrative. Here we have the full account of both trials in chapters 6 and 8, which includes the nail-biting attempt to get an eleventh-hour reprieve for one of the three condemned men as they are prepared to go to the rope. I won't reveal the result at this early stage.

PUNISHMENT

Just as crimes tend to be an indictment of the society in which they occur, so do the punishments that follow them, and the nineteenth century, and indeed the one before it in England, had some very severe sentences.

In modern Britain, imprisonment is the harshest sanction available, but this has not always been the case. Prison was just one of a number of sanctions available to the courts to deal with those who committed criminal offences. Prison as a punishment is not yet 200 years old; before this, in England at least, prison was either a place for keeping offenders before they were tried, transported or executed, or to prevent people from harming the government. Men and women, boys and girls, debtors and murderers were all held together in local prisons or perhaps prison hulks, which were old ships anchored in the Thames, off Portsmouth or Plymouth. Those sent to them were employed in hard labour during the day and then loaded, in chains, onto the ship at night. The appalling conditions on the hulks, especially the lack of control and poor physical conditions, eventually led to the end of that practice.

TRANSPORTATION

Sentencing a convicted person for transportation to a distant land was common in England for both petty and major crimes, and we will delve deeper into a few cases later on. In 1833, for a quick example, Thomas Alsop, labourer, was transported to Australia for seven years for stealing a pair of shoes. Elizabeth Archer received the same punishment four years later for taking six printed crape handkerchiefs and six shawls; either case could have easily appeared in one of Mr Dickens' novels.

Police constable with four felons, 1860.

This form of punishment commenced in the early 1600s, and continued well into the nineteenth century. A sentence could be for life or for a specified period, as we have just seen. Convicts would work on government projects, such as road building or mining, or were assigned to free individuals as unpaid labourers. Women were expected to work as domestic servants and farm labourers.

North America was used as a destination in the early years, and then, after the American War of independence, the ships were generally sent to Australia. In 1787, the first fleet set off for that distant country to found the first colony. The arrival at Port Jackson on 26 January 1788 (Australia Day) is now considered the founding event of the history of Sydney.

Transportation could have been a wonderful way to reform people if it had only been organised properly. Men and women who knew how to farm would have been ideal candidates; however, many pitiable creatures were sent away who had little chance of survival. Out of the first shipload of 600, only 200 survived the long and hazardous journey, plagued with scurvy and other vicious diseases. The ships themselves were in a poor state, while the food and water were almost rotten. Many of those who did make it were unfit for work on arrival. The second convoy was even worse, as hardened contractors used by an equally callous government were paid £17 for each convict taken on board. There was an obvious temptation to save money on food, as there were no deductions for delivering a corpse, or indeed many corpses.

This process of dispatching criminals to a variety of countries continued until the middle of the 1800s, at which time, many came to ask the question – what was the punishment in sending people out to a land when ordinary free labourers were keen to go for the opportunities that that land offered? Tasmania was then used until the prisoners outnumbered the free population by two to one. Nevertheless, in earlier times, transportation was a feared punishment, and some would have preferred to have hanged than go there.

CAPITAL PUNISHMENT

A tree was the earliest form of gallows, with prisoners being either hauled up manually by the hangman or turned off from a ladder or the tail of a cart. Two trees with a beam between them formed the gallows for thirty-three-year-old Mary Blandy's execution at Oxford on 6 April 1752.

In other places, more conventional gallows were built, having either a single upright with a projecting beam cross braced to it or two uprights and a cross beam where more than one person could be hanged at a time. Both types still required the use of a ladder or a cart to get the criminal suspended. Many of these gallows were not permanent and were dismantled after each execution. In some cases, the gallows was erected near to the scene of the crime so that the local inhabitants could see justice done.

THE OLD BAILEY

Several cases appearing in this book were tried at the Old Bailey. Bailey derives from the old fortified walls that used to stand there – a bailey was part of a castle's defences.

The modern building was built on the site of the infamous Newgate Prison and is the central criminal court of the United Kingdom. The Crown Court that operates there

Fradley Junction on the Trent & Mersey Canal, where the Pickford boatmen were held for some time following the discovery of the body of Christina Collins. (Robin Horton)

Lady Justice stands on top of the present Old Bailey. (Robert Deakin)

deals with major crimes committed in Greater London and, in exceptional cases, from other parts of the UK, such as the poisoner Doctor William Palmer. It was believed that he would not get a fair trial at Stafford, so the case was moved to London.

The original medieval court was first mentioned in the time of Queen Elizabeth I, and it was destroyed in the Great Fire of London in 1666. The court was rebuilt in 1674 and left open to the weather, as its designers tried to prevent the spread of disease. In 1734, it was enclosed and received a new front, after which an outbreak of typhus brought about the death of sixty persons, including the Lord Mayor and two judges. It was rebuilt again in 1774, and a second courtroom was added in 1824. Outside, on the dome above the court, is the famous Lady Justice designed by F. W. Pomeroy. She holds a sword in her right hand denoting power and authority to punish and a pair of scales denoting justice in her left.

OLD BAILEY FACTS

The court has popularly appeared in the works of Charles Dickens, for example, in *A Tale of Two Cities*, and in films such as *Witness for the Prosecution* with Charles Laughton and *Patriot Games* with Harrison Ford, and of course,

Trial at the Old Bailey.

The Old Court, Old Bailey. (C. McCutcheon)

Above: Exercise ground for condemned men, from the 'Glimpses of Old Newgate' series of postcards. (C. McCutcheon)

Right: Mrs Fry's Gate and Exercise Ground. Elizabeth Fry (1780-1845) was an English prison reformer who, in 1817, helped found the Association for the Reformation of the Female Prisoners in Newgate. (C. McCutcheon)

Visiting box and exterior of the scaffold at Newgate. (C. McCutcheon)

Rumpole of the Bailey, and more recently, *Garrow's Law* – BBC. Newgate Prison also featured in Charles Dickens' writings, and here he describes a visit to the gaol:

From this lodge, a heavy oaken gate, bound with iron, studded with nails of the same material, and guarded by another turnkey, opens on a few steps, which terminate in a narrow and dismal stone passage, running parallel with the Old Bailey, and leading to the different yards, through a number of tortuous and intricate windings, guarded in their turn by huge gates and gratings, whose appearance is sufficient to dispel at once the slightest hope of escape that any new-comer may have entertained; and the very recollection of which, on eventually traversing the place again, involves one in a maze of confusion.

It is necessary to explain here, that the buildings in the prison, or in other words the different wards – form a square, of which the four sides abut respectively on the Old Bailey, the old College of Physicians (now forming a part of Newgate Market), the Sessions House, and Newgate Street. The intermediate space is divided into several paved yards, in which the prisoners take such air and exercise as can be had in such a place. These yards, with the exception of that in which prisoners under sentence of death are confined, run parallel with Newgate Street, and consequently from the Old Bailey, as it were, to Newgate Market. The women's side is in the right wing of the prison nearest the Sessions House. As we were introduced into this part of the building first, we will adopt the same order, and introduce our readers to it also.

Turning to the right, then, down the passage to which we just now adverted, omitting any mention of intervening gates – we came to a door composed of thick bars of wood, through which were discernible, passing to and fro in a narrow yard, some twenty women: the majority of whom, however, as soon as they were aware of the presence of strangers, retreated to their wards. One side of this yard is railed off at a considerable distance, and formed into a kind of iron cage, about five feet ten inches in height, roofed at the top, and defended in front by iron bars, from which the friends of the female prisoners communicate with them. In one corner of this singular-looking den, was a yellow, haggard, decrepit old woman, in a tattered gown that had once been black, and the remains of an old straw bonnet, with faded ribbon of the same hue, in earnest conversation with a young girl – a prisoner, of course – of about two-and-twenty. It is impossible to imagine a more poverty-stricken object, or a creature so borne down in soul and body, by excess of misery and destitution, as the old woman.

... A little farther on, a squalid-looking woman in a slovenly, thick-bordered cap, with her arms muffled in a large red shawl, the fringed ends of which straggled nearly to the bottom of a dirty white apron, was communicating some instructions to her visitor – her daughter evidently. The girl was thinly clad, and shaking with the cold. Some ordinary word of recognition passed between her and her mother when she appeared at the grating, but neither hope, condolence, regret, nor affection was expressed on either side. The mother whispered her instructions, and the girl received them with her pinched-up, half-starved features twisted into an expression of careful cunning. It was some scheme for the woman's defence that she was disclosing, perhaps; and a sullen smile came over the girl's face for an instant, as if she were pleased: not so much at the probability of her mother's liberation, as at the chance of her 'getting off' in spite of her prosecutors. The dialogue was soon concluded; and with the same careless indifference with which they had approached each other, the mother turned towards the inner end of the yard, and the girl to the gate at which she had entered.

CHAPTER 2

Misdemeanours and Transportation

In this first section, we commence with what we might term small crime, committed between 1826 and 1842. All seven cases are heard at the Old Bailey and consist of four men and six women. This ratio is random, and in no way tries to put an entirely new meaning on the word miss-demeanour. Even though they may be small crimes, the punishment in some cases was by no means trivial. We soon discover that drinking is at the root of some of the problems, and boatmen should have been more careful of the female company that they kept, especially when known as 'Deaf Poll'. Policemen too needed to be extremely careful, as it appears that London girls were fond of biting them. Perhaps they tasted good! But oh, if only we could find so many constables on the beat today! As a monetary reference point, one guinea (one pound and a shilling) was pretty much what a common labourer, or boatman for that matter, would earn in a week.

Our first case is of **William John Shaw**, aged sixteen, who, in 1842, was caught for stealing – or technically referred to as simple larceny. On 22 August of that year, he was indicted for stealing one pair of trousers, value one shilling, a shirt with the same value, two handkerchiefs, value two shillings, and seven shillings in cash. This was the property of one Frederick Cooper, whose handkerchiefs were worth as much as his trousers.

So, let us imagine a typically hot summer's day in August. Frederick Cooper, who lives in Steven Street, Bethnal Green Road, has been strolling along the canal watching all the goings on, sees a few others swimming in the canal – they did in those days – and decides to join them. He takes off all his clothes, except his underpants of course (he's a modest sort of chap) and goes for a dip. The water is cool and refreshing, and he swims around for a while. But, when he gets out, he discovers to his shock and dismay that some swine has stolen his clothes, along with his money.

Fortunately for him, the perpetrator of this heinous crime is not very bright, just in need of some clothes and any odd cash lying around. William Shaw has not gone far and has been seen by an onlooker. As Cooper climbs out of the water, he immediately bumps into this onlooker and asks if he has seen anyone taking a bundle of clothes from that spot. The witness replies that he has, and he points to Shaw, who is sitting some way off on a fence that separates a field from the path leading down to the canal. Cooper cries 'STOP THIEF' and goes bombing off down the towpath after the culprit, wearing only a soggy pair of underpants. Shaw, not the most observant teenager, and more taken with going through the pockets of his newly purloined belongings than watching out for either the robbed or the law, is quickly apprehended by not one, but two policemen. Cooper, when put in the witness box claimed that he lost seven

Hangings taking place at Newgate.

shillings, and *6s* 10½*d* was found on Shaw – pretty close – while his handkerchief and clothes were soon recovered. The first witness was William Catlin.

William Catlin. I heard a cry of 'Stop thief' – I saw the prisoner running – I ran after him – I saw him drop this handkerchief – I picked it up, and gave it to the officer.

William French (police-constable). I took the prisoner – I found 10½*d* in his right hand.

George Kemp (police-constable). I went in pursuit of the prisoner – we caught him at Cambridge Heath Bridge – I laid hold of one hand, and my brother officer the other – In the lining of the waist of his trowsers I found six shillings – as we were going to search him, he said, 'You have no occasion to search me, I will give it up,' and he did.

William Edward Ball (police-constable). I produce a certificate of the prisoner's former conviction, which I got from Mr. Clark's office – *(read)* – the prisoner is the person.

The judge did not take long to reach a conclusion and the verdict was – unsurprisingly – GUILTY. William John Shaw was Transported for Seven Years in a Convict Ship.

Our second case involves two women, **Mary Thomas** and **Mary Smith,** who on 4 July 1833 were indicted for pickpocketing to the total of twelve sovereigns, the monies of Samuel Farrington. Our first witness – a boatman.

Samuel Farrington. I am a canal boatman. On Wednesday, the 19th of June, I was in town – I did not know either of the prisoners before; but I was at the Castle that night having a drop of beer, after we had cleared our boat, and I was too late to get into the yard; I then fell in with the prisoner Smith, and we went to the Leopard; when we got there, there were some loose men about, and as I had some money with me, the landlord advised me to leave my money with him, which I did – Smith was there with me at the time, but Thomas was not – I gave the landlord thirteen sovereigns and a half – I suppose it was ten or eleven o'clock, or it might be after; Smith still kept in company with me, and we went to Thomas's house, No. 7, Ball Yard – I cannot tell whether I saw Thomas there that night, as it was late – I cannot tell; we did not have any liquor there that I know of – I slept there, and I believe Smith slept with me; I found her aside of me the next morning – I got up in the morning and wanted my money, and Smith went with me to fetch it; I received it about eight o'clock – Smith and I had a little something to drink there, and we went back – I did not feel well by a great deal, and I said, I would go back and lay down upon the bed a little bit; I went back and laid down on the same bed I believe – I had my money in my breeches pocket – I had seen Thomas in the house that morning, and I fancy I gave her something to drink – Thomas was not in the room where I laid down; as Smith and I went up by ourselves up two pair of stairs – I don't know whether it was a room that Smith used or not – I laid down with my clothes on, and Smith as well; I fell asleep, and slept for about an hour; I then awoke, Smith was still on the bed, and I did not offer to awake her – I did not notice whether she was asleep or not, but I went down as fast as I could, as I found my pocket had been cut and the money gone out – I went down, but Thomas was not there – I sat down considering what I must do; after a while, the policeman came in and said, he had taken the woman that had got my money, and I went to Worship Street – I went to sleep that night at the Castle, and the next morning, when I got up and was dressing myself, my purse laid on the floor with a sovereign and a half in it – I had put my money into my purse when I received it of the landlord; I suppose they had taken the purse out of my pocket, and left me the sovereign and a half to do what I liked with – I believe the prisoners are the women.

Cross-examined by Mr Barry. Q. You are not quite sure they are the women?

Farrington. Yes, they are the women – I was not very drunk when I got to the Leopard – I was middling – I don't justly know where I met Smith, but we went to the Leopard together, and we went there again in the morning; we had not drank anything till we got there – I think I had half a pint of beer there – I did not sup the night before with these women, and have fish for supper – I did not give Thomas my money to take care of for me.

Joseph Crane. I keep the Leopard public-house in Seward Street, Goswell Street. On the Wednesday evening the prosecutor came to my house with two other men and two females – Smith was one of them, but Thomas was not – the prosecutor was not very tipsy; he called for half a pint of gin, which I served him with; he took his purse out to pay for it, and dropped his purse on the floor; I could tell by the sound that there was a good bit of money in it – I called him into the bar and persuaded him to leave his money till the morning, as he was rather in liquor, which he refused to do – but after a good deal of persuading he did, and went away; he wanted more liquor, which I refused to let him have – on the Thursday morning, he came in company with Smith, between eight and nine o'clock, for his money, I counted it out, and gave it him, there were thirteen sovereigns and a half; he had had fourteen sovereigns the night before, and changed one half sovereign to pay for what he had to drink.

Thomas Middlesex (police-constable). On Thursday afternoon, the 20th of June, a man came down and said, there was a woman with a great deal of property about her, and she had dropped four sovereigns and some silver on the ground; I went out with Kelly, and found Thomas standing drunk against the wall, between four and five o'clock – Kelly left me to go after a woman who they thought had been robbing Thomas, but I sung out for him to return to me, as Thomas began to bite me – we took her to the station-house; in going along she said, 'It was not me that robbed the Captain, it was Deaf Poll;' I began to search Thomas and four sovereigns fell from her – we searched her further, and found another sovereign on her, and four sovereigns and a half in the corner of her handkerchief, and some silver and copper in her pocket, amounting altogether to £10 11s 0¼d; there were nine sovereigns and a half in gold, one pound in silver and one shilling, and a farthing in copper.

Thomas Kelly (police-constable). I was with Middlesex; what he has stated is correct – I knew who was meant by Deaf Poll; Smith goes by that name.

Henry Beresford (police-sergeant). On the Thursday afternoon, Thomas and two other women were brought in; the money was found on Thomas as has been described – when the four sovereigns fell from her, I asked her if that was all she had, and she distinctly said, Yes; she was then searched and the rest of the money was found – she said, 'Deaf Poll took it and gave it me' – I went out, and from what I heard, I went to No. 7, Ball Yard (I asked her if she lived there? she said, Yes), I found the prosecutor there dozing; I asked him if he had been robbed? he said, Yes, of all his money – I took him to the station-house, and he identified Thomas; and before the Magistrate he stated the same – I searched him on the Thursday, but did not find any money, but I suspect the purse, with the sovereign and a half in it, had slipped down his trousers – he went to sleep that night at the Castle, and told me the next morning, that he found his purse and the sovereign and half on the floor.

Mary Thomas's Defence. He gave me the money, and told me to go for some fish, as I went I met two women who saw me drunk and wanted to take it from me – the prosecutor told me to keep the money for him; he kept a sovereign and a half, which he put into his purse – he was drunk when he gave it me.

Samuel Farrington. No, I don't recollect it; I should not have begun feeling for my money when I awoke if I had – I believe Smith is innocent.

Mary Thomas, aged forty, and Mary Smith, twenty-one, were both found guilty. The court records do not say what punishment they received.

Next we have another two women, **Elizabeth Sedley** and **Maria Potter**, and another Mary Smith, also charged with pickpocketing goods on 2 February, four sovereigns, and one half sovereign, the monies of Thomas Wright, from his person, on 14 February 1833. Our first witness again is a boatman, but this time originates from the Midland salt town of Droitwich. Again, drink gets in the way, and a boatman gets a night's 'female comfort' for three shillings. One of our 'ladies' seems to have thought that hiding the money in her mouth was a good idea!

Thomas Wright. I am a canal boatman, and live at Droitwich, in Worcestershire. On the night of the 2nd of February I went to the British Lion, in the City Road; my mate was with me – Sedley and Potter came in – one of the company asked them to drink, and they had some beer at my expence; I then sent my mate to see to my horse, and when he returned, he brought some empty bottles back for me – Sedley asked me what I was going to do with them; I said, 'To take some gin to some of my neighbours;' she said I should not have them filled there, she could take me to a place where I could get it better and cheaper – I then went with her, Potter, and my mate, to another public-house, where I got them filled; I had some gin and cloves there – Sedley, Potter, and my mate, had some rum; we then all went to the prisoners' house – I agreed to give Sedley 3 shillings to sleep with her: we had some more gin and cloves there, and I and Sedley went into a bed, in which there was another woman – I had put my waistcoat and breeches under the pillow, in which I had my pocket-book, with a £5 note, and four sovereigns and a half, and some silver wrapped up; I cannot tell whether I put out the candle or Sedley, but, after we had been some time in bed, Sedley had one arm under my head, and the other over me – I heard some handling of paper: I then listened and heard my pocketbook drop on the floor; I made an excuse that I wanted to get up, to which she objected, but I did get out, and, on getting out, I trod on my waistcoat, took it up, and the pocketbook was not in it; I then felt on the floor, and found my pocket-

Courtroom scene.

book open – I called my man, and said, 'I am robbed;' he came into the room – we looked, and found the £5 note in my pocket, but the sovereigns, and half sovereign, were gone; Potter then came into that room, but I did not see Smith till after the officer came – neither Smith nor Potter were in the room when I lost my money; I opened the window, and called Police! two sovereigns were afterwards found on Potter, and one sovereign in Smith's mouth, but that was in the lower room – I am positive it was Sedley took my money; I think it must have been conveyed to the other; when my man and Potter came up, I had charged Sedley with having my money, and she said, 'Search your pockets' – I felt, and found the £5 note, and some silver loose in my pocket.

John Hayford (Police-constable). I was on duty, and went to the house in Garden Row, between two and three o'clock in the morning. I saw the prosecutor calling out of the window – the door was opened; I went up stairs, and found Sedley, Potter, and another female in the room; the prosecutor said he had been robbed of four sovereigns and a half – I asked where it was; they said they had never seen it; Sedley said, if I would go about my duty, they would make it all right with the boatman – I then attempted to search them; they objected – I sprang my rattle, and Colee came to my assistance; we got them down stairs, and after a great struggle, I found one sovereign on Potter, and Colee found another – Potter kicked me and bit me very much; I found nothing on Sedley.

Henry Colee (Police-constable). I assisted this officer to search Potter – I found a sovereign between her shift and stays – that was in the lower room; I saw Smith sitting on the bed, and she had a sovereign in her mouth – I charged her with it, and it was gone, but it was afterwards found close by the bed, in the lower room.

Smith. You did not see it in my mouth?

Colee. Yes, I did.

Frederick Miles (Police-serjeant). I went to the house, and found a woman ill – I told her to go to bed, which she did, I then found two half-crowns on the cushion she had sat on.

Sedley's Defence. I went to the British Lion, and saw the prosecutor sitting there – he asked me to drink some half-and-half, which I did, and so did Potter; he then sent his mate for two bottles, and asked where he could get good gin – some person said at the Weaver's Arms, and we went there, and had seven quarters of gin – we came out, and he wanted me to go home with him, but I refused, as he had a wife and family, but at last I took him home; after some time, he said he had lost some money – I said, 'Get out and look for it,' which he did, but there was none there.

Potter's Defence. The two sovereigns found on me were given me by a young man – one was for myself, and one for him to buy some shirts; I was not in the room where the prosecutor was – his mate was in the room close to me, and must have seen if any money passed between us.

The Verdict – Elizabeth Sedley, aged twenty, and Maria Potter, aged twenty-two, were found guilty and sentenced to transportation for seven years. Mary Smith was found not guilty.

Elizabeth Lamb, aged twenty-eight, is our last 'lady' indicted for theft – pickpocketing one sovereign, one crown-piece, and three shillings, the monies of Richard Welch from his person. The case was held on 19 September 1836, and brought before Mr Justice Basanquet. Our first witness – again a boatman – didn't they have something better to do than catch criminals?

Richard Welch. I am a boatman at Paisley, in Staffordshire, in the employ of Messrs. Pickford. On Saturday the 3rd of September I was at the house of Ann Hixson, and saw the prisoner there – I did not know her before – I had no drink myself – half-a-gallon of beer was fetched into the house – I took two sixpences out of my purse, I had a sovereign, a crown-piece, and three shillings in it – the prisoner was present – I do not know whether she could see the money – the purse was in my left-hand

The Old Bailey. (Photo by Alison Stewart)

trowsers pocket – I had been drinking before, but had no beer there – I fell asleep in the room, and slept perhaps for three or four hours – the prisoner did not leave before I went to sleep – she was gone when I awoke, and my money was gone – there were others in the room besides the prisoner at the time I went to sleep – I found they were all gone – I gave an alarm about it, and went to search for the prisoner – I saw her late at night against Ann Hixson's door – I asked Hixson if Lamb was the woman I had been seeking, as I was not quite sure – Hixson said she was, and accused her about the money – the prisoner denied it several times – I threatened to fetch the police if she did not give it up – she then gave me 5s 6d and cried, and said that was all she had got – she said he had been to the fair, and spent 10s, and did not know what had become of the rest – she did not mention what fair – after she gave me the 5s 6d, I said if she would make it up to 10s, and make it up 10s more when I came from my next voyage I would make no more bother about it – she kept telling me she had got no more – she went to the top of the stairs – I thought she was going to get money down to make up the 10s, and asked her if she was going to get me any more – she made use of bad language, and told me to come up stairs, and take it out of her, if I wanted any more – I fetched a policeman, and gave her into custody.

Ann Hixson. I am a laundress, and wash for the carriers. I live in Hull Terrace St. Luke's – the prosecutor came to my house on Saturday the 3rd of September – the prisoner was there at the time – he produced a purse – every body present could see he had money – he went to sleep – the prisoner was still there – she sat right opposite him – I was tired myself and went to lie down leaving her in care of the place – after lying down a little while I heard somebody come into my room, and thought it was the prosecutor – I turned my head, and saw the prisoner rising up from the side of his person – from the front of him – there was a bed in my room, on which I was, and I thought she was taking the boots from under my bed – she went up into her own room, and shortly after she came down and said she was going to the fair – Welch was asleep when she got up from him, and slept some hours – the prisoner asked me to go to the fair, but I refused – when Welch awoke, he asked me for a light to go to the water-closet – I gave him a candle, and when he returned, accused me of the money – after eleven o'clock at night the prisoner knocked at the door – Welch met her on the step of the door, and asked if Lamb was the person we had been looking after – I said she was – I then accused her of the money and begged her to give it up, if she knew about it – she denied it very much at first, but at last said, 'I have robbed you, and am sorry for it, and 5s 6d is all I have got:' and she gave him the 5s 6d – he said, if he would make it up to 10s, and promise in my presence to pay 10s more he would freely forgive her, rather than neglect his work – she said she had no more – that she had been to the fair with George, who she lives with, and had spent the other – she went up stairs, and I heard her say what the prosecutor has stated – I fetched a policeman.

Hannah Johnson. I keep an eating-shop in John's Row at the fair time – the prisoner came there to sup on Saturday, the 3rd of September – there was a boatman with her – the supper came to 1s 2d, and she gave me a sovereign or half-sovereign, I am not certain which.

Elizabeth Lamb. It was a half-crown.

Hannah Johnson. I am quite sure it was gold.

Matthew Peak. I am a policeman. I was sent for to Mrs. Hixson's – an officer had been there before – Welch said if the prisoner would give him a sovereign, he would make it up – she said, if he would wait till Monday, she would pawn her gown to make up the rest of the sovereign – there was 6d in halfpence on the table, she said it was all she had – I found 6s in a band-box in her room – she said she had pawned her husband's shirt for that.

Daniel Collins. I am a policeman. I took Lamb into custody – I went up to the room where she was in bed – she produced 1s 6d in copper, and said she did not rob him.

Elizabeth Lamb's defence. I never touched a farthing of money out of his pocket – I went to take the boots – there are many persons in the house besides me – I never said I was going to the fair.

GUILTY. Aged 28. – Transported for Fourteen Years.

Our next case is that of **William Hancock**, aged nineteen, who, on 14 September 1826, was charged with stealing – 19 yards of cloth, value £15; 74 yards of kerseymere, value £22, and one wrapper, value 6d, the goods of Zachary Langton, and others, his partners, to whom he was a servant.

Robert Lambert. I am in the employ of Pickford and Co. – Zachary Langton is one of the partners. I saw this bale of goods at Bow Street – the prisoner has been in our employ three or four years – we pay the Captain, who pays him.

Thomas Wise. I am a porter at Messrs. Pickford's. I remember a bale of goods coming, directed to Mr. Slater, Knutsford; I saw it opened the next day, and it contained seventy-six yards of kerseymere in one wrapper – it was brought to our warehouse from the Castle inn, Wood Street, on the 3rd of August; I saw it in the warehouse – it was to go to Knutsford, by Pickford and Co.'s canal boat. It was the duty of the shipping clerk to put it on board; the prisoner was boatman to Messrs. Pickford and Co.; this truss was to have gone by a Liverpool boat; I saw the prisoner going across the warehouse with it – he had no business with it, because he was not loading that boat then – this was about nine o'clock at night; I was at work in the warehouse, and he set the truss against the door, near the scale where they weigh the goods; I went out, and when I returned I saw the prisoner – the truss was gone; I went up to the door to see where he was gone with it, and he was carrying it in his

Pickford's boats in double lock. (A. Faulkner)

arms, up to the far end of the boat – it fell into the water – he took it up, and put it in a place where they put coals – not where they put goods – when he came back I asked what he had been at, and what that was which he let fall in the water; he said he supposed it was a block fell off the boat; I then went and told the gentleman of it – they came out and we went and pulled the boat back, and found the truss – the prisoner was then gone out.

Edward Powner. I am clerk to Messrs. Pickford and Co. The prisoner was a boatman – it was not his duty to remove this truss – he had nothing to do with it; on Thursday evening Wise said they had got something in the boat which they had no business with; I went and took it out, and saw the direction on it; it was not to have gone by that boat – it was loading for Leicester; the prisoner belonged to that boat; the bale was found among the coals – not a proper place to stow goods; I saw it opened afterwards – it contained seventy yards of kerseymere.

Robert Lambert. This kerseymere is worth £22, and the broad-cloth £15 – making £37 together.

John Church. I am a porter. The prisoner gave me 6d to go and get a drop of beer, and while I was gone he made away with the truss.

Alexander Moore. Policeman. I was sent for, and took the prisoner; he said he knew nothing about it.

GUILTY. Aged 19. Transported for Seven Years.

We close this chapter with another two minor crimes, though it is difficult to understand why Thomas Lucas was only given six months imprisonment and not seven years transportation. Perhaps there were worries that Australia was filling up, but it is more likely due to the fact that Lucas 'came quietly' and returned the stolen property. Contrast that, if you will, to our final case, Thomas Hughes, who after being apprehended for stealing only a bridle, receives a year in gaol, along with a whipping. It makes you wonder what he would have received for a similar crime today; a warning at the police station – maybe?

Thomas Lucas was tried for theft on 31 December 1838.

Thomas Lucas was indicted for stealing, on the 20th of December, 1 jacket, value 2s; 1 handkerchief, value 2s; 1 flannel shirt, value 1s; 2 pairs of stockings, value 1s; and 2 shirts, Value 2s; the goods of John Corry: 1 razor, value 6d; 1 shirt, value 1s; 1 pair of trowsers, value 1s; and 1 pair of stockings, value 2s; the foods of James Wagstaff: 1 waistcoat, value 12s; 1 tea-caddy, value 6d; ¼ lb weight of tea, value 1s 6d; and ¾ lb weight of cheese, value 4d; the goods of Ralph Loundes, in a certain boat on the Navigable Grand Junction Canal.

John Corry. I am a boatman, belonging to *The Jane*, lying in the Grand Junction Canal, at Paddington. I, Wagstaff, and Taylor, kept our things in the cabin-cupboard – I saw mine safe last Thursday week – I went to a beer-shop about six o'clock that evening, with Wagstaff – the prisoner came in, and sat by my side – I knew him before – he is a boatman out of employ – he had a silk handkerchief in his breast, which I knew to be mine – I did not then know the boat was robbed, but Wagstaff went out, came back, and gave me information – I then pulled the handkerchief out of the prisoner's breast, and asked what he had there – he said, 'Nothing' – I said it was mine, and if he would tell me where the other property was, I would let him at liberty – he said he would not tell me, but he would show me where they were – he took me and my captain, Ralph Loundes, to a beer-shop in Praed Street, and asked the landlord for a bundle, which he gave him – it contained a shirt of Wagstaff's, and a pair of stockings of mine – I asked where the other property was, and he sent me with a police-man to another beer-shop – we found another bundle there containing this jacket of mine, a razor of Wagstaff's, and two shirts of Taylor's – I have lost two shirts, one flannel shirt, and a silk handkerchief entirely.

(Property produced and sworn to.)

David Turner (police-constable). I was called into the beer-shop in Praed Street, and found the prisoner there – the landlord said the prisoner had left this bundle – the prisoner did not deny it – it contains shirts, stockings, and the tea-caddy.

James Wagstaff. I belong to *The Jane*. I left my property safe in the cabin-cupboard – this bundle contains some of it – I have got all mine back.

GUILTY. Aged 23. – Confined Six Months.

And finally, Thomas Hughes' case was heard on 30 October 1811.

Thomas Hughes was indicted for feloniously stealing, on the 34th [*sic*] of September 1811, a bridle, value 8*s*, the property of John Boswell.

John Boswell. I am a boatman. I live at Birmingham. I lost my bridle out of Mr. Crab's stable, at Paddington. From information I went to the Red Lion, at Kilburn. I found the bridle on the horses head, of the man that bought it, his name is John Thorn.

John Thorn. I am a higler. The prisoner said to me, countryman, I will sell you a saddle and bridle. We went up to the Star & Garter. Boswell enquired if his brother had left the house. Those at the Star & Garter said yes. Boswell then said – The saddle has already gone. I will sell you the bridle for three shillings. I said I will give you half a crown if you will take it to a sadler's, so he took it to a sadler's, there I bought it. I would not buy it without a witness. I am sure he is the man. This is the bridle.

Boswell. That is my bridle, it is marked J. B. inside the winkers.

Prisoner's Defence. I never saw any thing of it.

GUILTY, aged 30.

Confined one Year in the House of Correction, and whipped in jail.
Second Middlesex jury, before Mr. Recorder.

CHAPTER 3

Violent Assault

The cases, and thus the trials, now grow longer, with increased witness testimonies as the crimes take on a more serious nature. Now we will see John Turfrey and Samuel Harding, indicted for violent theft on 14 February 1833, on Thomas Bodle, a boatman. It goes without saying that the punishments also step up a gear from this case onward.

Thomas Bodle, a boatman arriving in the capital to collect coal, does what most of his associates have done before him – he heads for the pub, but in his case several pubs. He starts drinking at 6.30 p.m., at the Windsor Castle with 2 to 3 quarts of porter, a glass of gin, followed by another pint or two of porter until 11.30, whilst singing a few songs. But he isn't finished yet! Thomas being made of stern stuff, transfers from the Castle to the Macclesfield Arms, where he downs another glass of gin, a glass of port wine, asks for more and is refused. Undeterred, he heads away to the City Arms, but by now, he can't really recall what, if anything, he had there. Let's follow the case:

Second Middlesex Jury, before Mr. Justice Patterson.

John Turfrey and **Samuel Harding** were indicted for feloniously assaulting Thomas Bodle, on the 3rd of February, at St. Luke, putting him in fear, and taking from his person, and against his will, 6 shillings, 5 sixpences, and 3 halfpence, his property.

Thomas Bodle. I am a boatman, and live at Ratcliff, near Nottingham – I am in the employ of Mr. Munday; I came from Shipley to London for coals – we came to London on the Friday before I was at the Police-office; I was at the Windsor Castle, City Road, on the Saturday, about six o'clock, or about half-past six in the afternoon; I drank there until half-past eleven o'clock; I remained there the whole time – Turfrey was drinking on the other side of the table I sat at; he did not drink with me – he was trying to sell something; I did not drink such a vast deal there; I was not at all drunk when I left there, nor was I the worse for liquor; I left the house, at half-past eleven o'clock – I wanted some more liquor, and they would not give it to me – I paid for what I had; I then had between 8s and 9s in my pocket in silver, and 1½d in copper – when I came out Turfrey followed me close – I went to the Macclesfield Arms, over the canal bridge, City Road; Turfrey came into the house after me – I had some drink there; I believe I had a glass of gin and a glass of red port wine; I wanted more there – they would not give it me; I left there, then went across the way to the City Arms, and did not see Turfrey go in there; I sat down and went to sleep there – I do not remember drinking anything there; I felt myself rather fresh when I was there – I do not know how long I slept there; the next I recollect was when I was walking

Typical noose used in British hangings of the late nineteenth and twentieth century.

on the bridge by myself (I do not recollect coming out of the house) – then Harding and Turfrey came up together; I had never seen Harding before, to my recollection – they came up and said, 'Lay hold of the b—r's hands, and let us take him on board;' Harding said so – my boat laid at the wharf No. 33 in the City Road, three or four hundred yards from the bridge; they were then taking me along the road – one laid hold of one arm, and one the other; they took me along the road till I showed them which wharf my boat laid down – they took me about halfway down the wharf.

I said I could go by myself then, and thanked them – they let go of me, and I was going to the boat by myself; they ran after me again, and said, 'Let us knock the b—r down and take his money from him;' Harding said that, and he ran up to me, hit me on the breast, and knocked me down – Harding put his hands into my breeches pockets, and then said, 'Lay hold of the b—r's legs, let us kill the b—r, and heave him in this hole; Turfrey was looking on – he was close to me when Harding struck me; Turfrey then laid hold of my legs, and Harding laid hold of my arms; they hove me right into a hole – it was like an unfinished building, like a cellar hole; I do not know how deep it was – I recollect nothing more till I found myself at the station-house on the Sunday morning; my money was not in my pocket then – the last place I saw my money at was the Macclesfield Arms; I took it out to pay there, and Turfrey saw me with it – the landlord said in his presence, that I had better have nothing to do with such a man as that, and told me to go and get a bed somewhere, or else go to my boat; I do not recollect what Turfrey said – he was jawing the landlord; this was inside the Macclesfield Arms – the landlord's man put him out of the house, before I went out; I then went to the City Arms – I do not recollect seeing Turfrey after I left the Macclesfield Arms, till he came up with Harding; I did not know him before that day – I had never seen either of them before; I swear Harding is the man – I was sober enough to speak to his features; it was a very light night, moon-light, as light as it is here almost.

Cross-examined by Mr Phillips. Q. Can you tell us how much you drank at the Windsor Castle?

Bodle. No, I had some porter – I cannot tell how much I paid for; I will swear it was not two or three quarts – I do not recollect what I drank next; I had a glass of gin, I believe there, and a pint or two of porter – I will not swear I did not drink four pints of porter; I might have a glass of gin or two – I do not know how much; I cannot recollect whether I had any thing else there – I do not think I had any wine, but am not certain; I believe I paid the man for what I had – I do not know whether he waited on me all the while; I may have paid a man and a woman – I paid for every thing as it was brought; I believe the last thing I had was gin – I was not drunk when I left the Windsor Castle; I saw the landlady at the City Arms – I was rather fresh when there, I believe; I was sensible.

Q. Perhaps then you recollect Turfrey requesting the landlady to give you a bed there, as you were so drunk?

Bodle. I cannot recollect it – I do not recollect seeing him there at all; I do not know at what time I left the City Arms – I do not recollect being taken out of that house by Harding in his arms; I recollect nothing till I found myself walking upon the bridge, which is forty or fifty yards from the house – I do not remember being outside the house by the shutters and falling down.

Q. Did you not tumble into the cellar yourself?

Bodle. No, when I awoke at the station-house, I was surprised to find myself there – I do not recollect saying I knew nothing about Harding.

John Groome. I am waiter at the Windsor Castle, City Road. On Saturday, the 2nd of February, I remember the prosecutor coming there, about six o'clock – he staid there and had a pint of beer, and went out again; I know Turfrey – he came in about half-past five o'clock, and was there when Bodle came in, and remained there; they were in the same room – Turfrey offered some seals for sale, while Bodle was there; he remained there all the time – Bodle came back about eight o'clock, had a pint more porter, and remained there smoking his pipe till about half-past nine o'clock, and was singing, and then he had a quartern of gin and some warm water; he sung

Newgate scene.
(L. Jackson)

several songs after that, till about half-past ten o'clock – then he had a glass of rum in some warm water, then he sat till about a quarter after eleven o'clock, and wanted another glass of rum in warm water – master said it was too late to serve, and would not serve him with any more; he paid for the liquor as he had it, except for the glass of rum – master told him it was half-past eleven o'clock, and it was time to go out; I told all the people it was time to go – Bodle was going out without paying for his rum; master called him back and he stood talking in the passage while I let Turfrey out, and when I opened the door to let Bodle out Turfrey stood at the door, and they walked off together – the prosecutor was not drunk; he was capable of knowing what he was doing – he was not sober.

Cross-examined. Q. How far is the Macclesfield Arms from your house?

Groome. One hundred yards.

Nicholas Lucraft. I keep the Macclesfield Arms. Bodle came into my house on the 2nd of February, a little before twelve o'clock, alone – Turfrey was there; I will not be certain which came in first – Bodle certainly had been drinking; he was not sober, but I think he knew what he was doing – he had a glass of gin put into some cold water; he paid for it – I saw 8s or 12s, in his hand when he paid me; he held it open in his hand for a minute – Turfrey was standing close by him, and saw it; the prosecutor asked me if he could have a bed at my house for the night – I said he could not, but I dare say he could get one in the neighbourhood; Turfrey told him he would give him a bed if he would go to Paddington with him – I told him he had better not go to Paddington, but get a bed in the neighbourhood, and desired him to have nothing to do with Turfrey, as he was a strange man; Turfrey did not like what I said, and got insolent to me – I ordered my servant to put him outside the door; and again told the prosecutor to have nothing to do with him; my servant took Turfrey by the arm, and rather lead him out of the house – Bodle stopped about two minutes, and then he went; I saw no more of it.

Cross-examined. Q. About what time did the prosecutor come to your house?

Lucraft. About five minutes to twelve o'clock – I thought before he went that he had had quite sufficient; I served him as I should another customer – I was preparing to clear my house; he had a glass of port wine almost immediately after the gin – he mixed it all up together – I did not say any thing to him about it; he did not walk out of my house like a tipsy man – he was not very drunk; the City Arms is about one hundred yards from my house.

Rachael Jones. I keep the City Arms. On the night of the 2nd of February the prisoner Turfrey came to my house – I never saw him before; it was about ten minutes or a quarter after twelve o'clock – he came into the house, and had half a pint of ale; Bodle came in five or ten minutes after – he staggered in, and the moment he got in he sat down on the bench by the bar, and said to Turfrey, 'Old fellow are you here, you shall have a glass of something to drink,' naming gin; Turfrey said he had rather not, he had got his ale, and would not take any thing more – Turfrey then came to me, and said, 'I have been in company with this man before this evening – he wants a bed;' Bodle was sitting close to him, and was awake then – I said nothing to that, and Turfrey said, 'He has got some money about him, I know, and if he will leave it with you, I will take him to Paddington to sleep;' I recollect nothing more – I made no answer about my taking the money, but some man at the bar said it would be as safe as if he had got it with him, if he left it with me, but I said nothing, he being a stranger – he fell asleep, fell under the bench, and laid there about twenty minutes, till I was about to clear the house; I requested somebody to go and take him up from the bench – Harding was the man who took him up – he was there when the prosecutor came in; he took him up several times, endeavouring to awake him, but could not – he was quite in a state of insensibility; I recollect nothing else – they took him outside the door, and I saw nothing more; this was about a quarter to one o'clock – it was some time before I could get him out of doors.

Cross-examined. Q. At the time he left your house was he not in such a state of drunkenness that you would not rely on any thing he either said or did?

Jones. I would not; I never saw a man more drunk in my life; I am sure Turfrey desired him to leave his money with me – I have known Harding four years – he is married, and has two children; he gets his living by working at the wharfs, or any thing he can get to do – I never heard any thing against his honesty; he frequented my house with a set of hard-working men.

COURT. Q. When this happened was he in work or not?

Jones. He had been at work that day at Green and Barrett's – I heard the men say so.

William Epps. I am a Policeman. On Saturday night, the 2nd of February, I was on duty in Wharf Road, City Road – part of my beat was in the City Road,

Typical boatman with his horse. Note that the horse is equipped with towing harness and large blinkers. The boatman has leather straps on his legs as was often the practice, as was wearing the neckerchief.

near the canal-bridge; I first saw Bodle between eleven and twelve o'clock that night, it was nearer twelve; Turfrey was walking about three feet from him – he and Bodle were walking up the City Road about three feet apart; I did not observe any other person – they went over the bridge, and I lost them; I saw the two prisoners and the prosecutor, about half-past two o'clock, just coming out of the City Road into the wharf road – Harding had hold of the prosecutor's right arm, and Turfrey his left arm, and as they went past me, Turfrey said to him, 'You make yourself drunker than you really are;' he said, 'You know I am your countryman and your friend, why don't you walk as you ought to do;' by his saying that, I thought it was not all right, and watched them; I went a little way from them, then turned back, followed them, and observed them in the yard of No. 33 wharf, all three together, but what they were doing I cannot say – Harding looked back, and then I popped behind a gate-post for them not to see me, and in about a quarter of a minute I looked again, and the prosecutor was missing; I did not know where he was gone to – the two prisoners were coming down the yard; Turfrey came out first, and Harding followed – Harding said to Turfrey, 'Are you going home?' Turfrey said Yes – Harding said, 'Good night,' and they parted; Turfrey went one way and Harding the other – Turfrey had not gone above ten yards before he turned and came back, and wanted to make me believe he was as drunk as he could be to walk – I went and met him, and he said, 'Have you seen any thing of a boatman?' I said No, I had seen no boatman, and as I told him that Harding came up (they at first were both going in a direction from me) – Harding said, 'Have you seen him?' Turfrey said, 'No, and the Policeman has not seen him.'

I then walked towards the City Road, a few yards away from them – they went towards the wharf No. 33 again together; I went and concealed myself behind a cart opposite the wharf gate – they came out of the yard again, looked about for a quarter of a minute, and Harding said to Turfrey, 'Let us go and see if we have done for the b—r;' Turfrey replied, 'If we have not, we soon will do;' they went back up the yard again – I observed my brother officer Cook coming up; I called for his assistance, and told him my suspicions; we were going towards the gateway, and met the prisoners just out of the gate – we went up to them, and I asked Harding what business he had up that yard – he told me he had not been up the yard; I told him I had seen him go up; he said he had not been up – I asked him where the countryman was – he said he knew nothing about the countryman, he had not seen him; I said, 'Then let us go back, and see if we can find him;' he said very well, and we all four went back, and Cook, looking into an unfinished house, with a cellar under it, said, 'Here he lays.'

I turned my lantern on, and saw him laying flat on his back in the cellar – I thought he was dead; we then got the two prisoners down to assist him up, for I did not like to go down myself, for fear they should escape – Cook said, 'Here is his pocket inside out;' it was his right-hand breeches pocket; I looked, and it was so – I then got the prosecutor up; I laid him down, sprang my rattle, and got more assistance – I said to Harding, 'It is my opinion you have robbed this man, and meant to murder him;' he said, 'No, I have not;' I said, 'I shall search you;' he said, 'You may search me, I have nothing about me;' I then searched him, and found six shillings, five sixpences, and 1½d – I asked him how he came by it; he said he earned 1s 5d that day, and afterwards that he had earned 1s 7d; I asked him how he got the rest – he said he should not satisfy me; we took them to the station-house, secured them, and then fetched the prosecutor – he could not walk; we were obliged to get a truck; we could not make any sense of him – I could not tell whether it was with liquor or from his fall; my brother officer searched the prosecutor.

Cross-examined. Q. When you first saw the prosecutor, he was walking as if he was drunk?

Epps. No, not when I saw him between eleven and twelve o'clock, but when I saw him near the wharf; I afterwards saw the two prisoners alone – they separated, went different ways, and then both came back to me.

Q. If conscious of having done wrong, was there any thing to prevent them going away?

Epps. No; I should have taken care that Turfrey did not go away – I was about five yards from him; he turned back and came to me.

Q. After that they were looking about for him?

Epps. They were looking for somebody – the cellar is six or eight feet deep; it is an open cellar – a drunken man might very readily tumble into it; he appeared to walk as if he was very drunk – he had the prisoners with him; the place is near the water – he might have fallen in if left alone. I thought it my duty to watch them, and not to go and inquire where he was going; the prisoners went down the cellar readily to help him up; Cook did not go down with them, he took hold of him as they lifted him up.

Q. If they were conscious of robbing him, might they not have put his pocket in before they lifted him up?

Epps. We should have seen it; Turfrey did not appear drunk when we got to the station-house.

JURY. Q. How far from the cellar did you last see the prisoners with the prosecutor?

Epps. Right opposite, about four yards, or not quite so far; I saw them all three together there – I did not see the prosecutor alone at all, till I found him in the cellar; they were all three standing still, opposite the cellar, when I last saw them, they were in the middle of the cart road, and after I had seen them together there I missed the prosecutor – the prisoners were then coming towards me; they could not get out without coming to me – I had lost sight of them for about a quarter or half a minute.

Old Bailey scene.

Q. When they returned and asked if you had seen the boatman, are you aware whether they knew you had overheard them?

Epps. I was close by them – they were not aware that I had seen them go up the yard a second time – they saw me going, as they thought, up the City Road; they both went down towards the yard; they were not aware that I overheard their conversation – it did not take half a minute to get behind the cart.

COURT. Q. If we understand you right, they separated once, and went different ways, neither of them then coming towards you?

Epps. No, but after that, Turfrey turned back and came and spoke to me – while he was talking, Harding also came up, and asked if he had seen him; I then turned from them and they went towards the yard – they could not then tell that I could see what they did, as I went and concealed myself behind the cart; it was moon-light.

Mr Phillips. Q. When you saw the three standing together, how near were you to them?

Epps. About five yards; it was moon-light – the wind blew very much, I could hardly hear any thing – it was a very boisterous night indeed: but I was not above two yards from them when I heard them speaking, and close to them when Turfrey said to the prosecutor, 'You are making yourself drunker than you are;' they could not avoid seeing me then.

COURT. Q. How near were you to them when they said, 'Let us go and see if we have done for him?'

Epps. About four yards.

William Cook. I am a Police-constable. On the Sunday morning, between two and three o'clock, my brother officer called me; I went with him to 33 Wharf, and when I was within nine or ten yards of the gate I met Harding, I walked up to him, and asked what he did up that wharf at that time in the morning; he said he had not been up the yard. I told him I saw him come out; while I was questioning him, Turfrey came out, and when he saw me, he asked me if I had seen a countryman of his; I asked him what countryman; he said, 'A boatman that he just took up the yard;' he said, 'We have been to look for him, but cannot find him.' I said to both the prisoners 'Go up the yard, and I will see whether I cannot find him;' we proceeded up the yard, about half way, and there is an unfinished building, and in the third opening there is a place dug out for a cellar, between five and six feet deep – I looked down, and observed the prosecutor laying on his back; I turned round to Harding, and said, here he is; he said, 'So he is;' my brother officer turned his light on, and I thought he was dead at first – I desired Turfrey to get down, which he did, and we sent Harding down – they lifted him up, I laid hold of his arms, dragged him up, laid him on the ground, and his right-hand breeches-pocket was turned inside out; my brother officer said he had been robbed – I said, 'Yes, it appears so;' I sprang my rattle twice, and another officer came up. I desired him to stand over the prisoners, while we laid the prosecutor in a shed – then we took the prisoners to the station, returned and fetched the prosecutor in a truck. I searched Turfrey on the spot, and found 1½d on him. I searched the prosecutor's pockets – he had no money at all, I did that when I came back to fetch him – in going to the station-house, Turfrey said he had nothing to do with leading the prosecutor down the Wharf Road. Harding turned round and said, 'Don't tell a falsehood, speak the truth – you know you was with me.'

Cross-examined. Q. Had you both the prisoners in charge at the time?

Cook. No; I had Turfrey, Epps and another officer had Harding on ahead of me, he might hear what Harding said – I should think he could not avoid it. Epps said the man had been robbed; I did not hear him say, 'In my opinion you have robbed

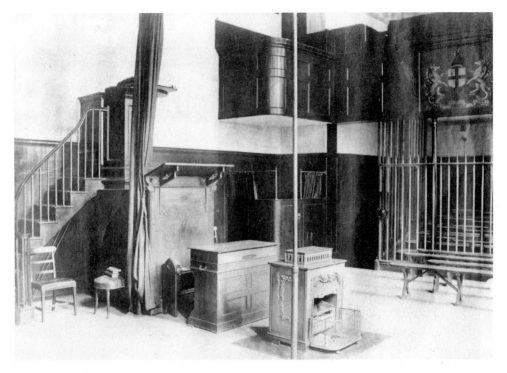

Interior of chapel at Newgate showing condemned seat. Turfrey and Harding would have been brought to this room prior to execution and visited by the chaplain. (C. McCutcheon)

The interior of the scaffold at Newgate. (C. McCutcheon)

The burial ground of executed prisoners at Newgate. (Images on these pages courtesy C. McCutcheon)

This bell was rung outside the condemned cell at Newgate at midnight on the eve of an execution. The bellman then recited the following verse:

All you that in the condemned hole do lie,
Prepare you, for tomorrow you shall die;
Watch all, and pray: the hour is drawing near,
That you before the Almighty must appear.

Examine well yourself; in time repent,
That you may not to eternal flames be sent,
And when St Sepulchre's bell in the morning tolls,
The Lord above have mercy on your souls.

the man first, and then intended to murder him.' I was not paying attention – I was three or four yards from him; I paid attention to some part of what he said, but might not hear all.

Turfrey's Defence. Gentlemen, I hope you will look into it; I am myself really as innocent as a new born babe, of either word, deed, or action, but kindness to the man, to get him a lodging.

Harding's Defence. I have had the distance measured from where the Policeman stood watching; it is fifty-eight feet from the hole – he was behind a cart which is across the road-outside the wharf; it is eighteen yards from the cart to the waggon inside the wharf, where he says we stood and made the expressions to each other. [...]

Two witnesses gave Turfrey a good character.

Feb. 15th – TURFREY – GUILTY – DEATH. Aged 24.
HARDING – GUILTY – DEATH. Aged 28.

Fortunately for our forgetful boatman, the whole sorry episode was seen and heard by the local bobbies; otherwise he may very well have died down in the cellar. Then again, it is obvious that after consuming so much alcohol he may not have felt a thing – he certainly seemed to recover quickly enough. In one way, we can feel a little sympathy for the two defendants that they received the death penalty for a paltry amount of money, but then again, Bodle could easily have been killed when they threw him down into the pit. The account does not tell us whether the pair did actually receive the punishment of death, because even though many were sentenced to such, a proportion did get a reprieve.

CHAPTER 4

Manslaughter

Manslaughter, or the accidental killing of a person, is the subject of chapter four, and I have three very different cases here for your perusal. Our first case all started off in a seemingly silly argument about who should fill a lock: ponder on that the next time you reach for your windlass. The second case is self-explanatory, though you may find some of the medical practices rather barbaric; while the third was caused by negligence, and not following the normal operating procedure for the passing of two horse boats.

CASE I
THE DEATH OF WILLIAM NORMAN

James Carpenter was tried for manslaughter on 26 October 1846.

James Carpenter was indicted for feloniously killing and slaying of **William Norman**.

Samuel Jordan. I am lock-keeper at the Grand Junction Canal, at Harefield. On Saturday morning, the 26th of Sept., the prisoner came to my lock – Norman was there – the prisoner came forward to pull the lock – the lock was not ready to receive the boats, and Norman asked the prisoner what was the reason he did not come sooner to get it ready – the prisoner and Norman worked in a different pair of boats, but both belonged to one master – they had words, and called each other liars, and then Norman called the prisoner some name that I could not understand – the prisoner answered, 'Can you make me one?' – Norman said yes, he could, and immediately threw off his cap, and doubled his fist to fight the prisoner – the prisoner had not then done anything, but called Norman names – they walked away from the lock, round the corner of the palings, where I could not see them, and were fighting for some minutes, and then I went over from my side of the lock, and told them they had a great deal better leave off fighting, and follow their boats; they had had enough of that I thought – the prisoner immediately said, 'That is just as he likes' – Norman made an answer which I was not near enough to understand – they went from there into the meadow, and were there some time – I was out of sight of them – I then went into the road, and saw Norman's brother trying to lift him up – his brother had repeatedly, in my hearing, begged him to leave off fighting – I could not hear what reply Norman made to that.

Cross-examined by Mr Ballantine. Q. Norman was a short stout man?

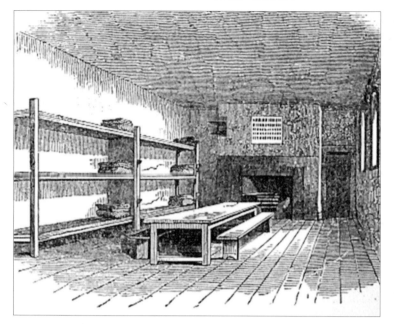

Newgate cell.
(L. Jackson)

Jordan. Yes, and he called the prisoner several names – it appeared to me that Norman was the person provoking the whole thing – the prisoner appeared to me to endeavour to get out of it – the next thing I found was that Norman was dead – I went to the meadow, and told his brother he was a corpse.

George Norman. I am the brother of William Norman, who died. The quarrel began about the lock not being ready – the prisoner said it was not his place to fill the locks – my brother told him it was – the prisoner said he was a liar – my brother said he was not, and he said, 'You are a liar, and a b—y liar' – the prisoner replied, 'Can you make one of me?' – my brother said, 'Yes,' and he threw off his cap, and doubled his fists, and began to square at him – I begged him not to fight at all – I said, 'There wants no fighting;' but he would, and he and the prisoner went down the road, a little distance from the lock.

I got my lines ready, and went down after them, they got into the meadow, and began fighting again – my brother pulled off his shirt – he would not leave off – the prisoner had pulled off his shirt in the road – I went into the field, and begged my brother to leave off – he struck at me, and said he would have another round or two – they began to fight again, and fought for ten minutes, I dare say – when my brother said he would have another round or two, the prisoner said as he liked about that – he seemed willing to give it up – they fought a few rounds, and in the last round my brother tumbled down backward, and lodged his elbow in the ground for a minute, and all at once he fell back like a person in a fit – he made a kind of gurgling in his throat, and I never heard any more from him.

Cross-examined. Q. When your brother struck at you he was exceedingly excited?

G. Norman. Yes – he had got several pieces of skin knocked off – he was very passionate – when my brother was dead the prisoner did not know it – he said 'I won't fight any more,' and he went off down to the boats – my brother drank a good deal at times.

Hayes Kidd. I am a surgeon – I was called upon to examine the body of William Norman – I found contusions about his face, but not, apparently, sufficient to cause death – I made a post mortem examination – I found the vessels of the brain in a highly congested state, and an extensive extravasation of blood in the ventricles of the brain – I considered the cause of death in the flow of blood into the brain.

Cross-examined. Q. He died, in point of fact, from apoplexy?

Kidd. No – I consider the rupture was occasioned by external violence – the vessels of the brain got very full of blood which caused congestion – there was a rupture – the flow of blood from the vessels to the brain was the cause of his death. The cause of the congestion might be extreme excitement – in making a blow at his brother he might have brought on the congestion which ultimately ended in the rupture, and being a person of intemperate habits the vessel were more likely to rupture than in any man of other habits.

Verdict – NOT GUILTY.

CASE 2

THE DEATH OF JOHN GOODWIN, BOAT BOY

In the nineteenth century, the canal was a busy place of legitimate work, even on a Christmas day, but it could also be the scene of a crime, injury and even death. This is the unfortunate story of a young boat boy who, during the winter of 1869/70, was cruelly mistreated by a boatman named William Parker. Parker may indeed have been a real brute, but then again he may have been no better or worse than many other boatmen of the time. There seems no doubt that Parker did indeed strike the boy, but was he really a murderer, or was the boy's death a result of the poor medical treatment of those times? I shall leave the conclusion to the reader. This is the account of the case.

On 11 March 1870, an inquest was held at a public house on Bath Row, Birmingham, regarding the unfortunate death of John Goodwin, a boat boy sixteen years of age. Presiding over the meeting was Dr John Birt Davies, Borough Coroner. The boy was the son of William Goodwin, farm labourer at Delvey's Green near Oldbury, and until the time of his death, he had been residing at the house of Sarah Hadley near the Blue Gates, Smethwick.

It had been alleged that the deceased had been subjected to some undue violence by a man with whom he worked named William Parker, boatman from the Blue Gates. The incident had occurred on Thursday 20 January at the side of the Birmingham/Walsall Canal near the Bridgeman Street Bridge, Walsall (by Walsall Town Wharf at the bottom of Walsall Locks), and the boy had finally died as a result of his injuries at the Queen's Hospital Birmingham. As a consequence, a warrant had been issued by Chief Superintendent Cater of Walsall for Parker's apprehension. The latter had been arrested and taken before the magistrates in Walsall and remanded to await the result of the inquest by the borough coroner.

The first witness to be called was Sarah Hadley, with whom the deceased had lodged for about five months. She said that, on 20 January, the boy returned home and complained of being extremely ill; in his own words, he said that he was afraid that he was going to have an attack of the rheumatism, similar to that which he had experienced some two years previously. On the same day, he sent out for two pennyworth of rum, which he drank neat. The next day he said that he was too ill to go to work and stayed at home. On the Saturday, he went out with a boat to work, but on the Sunday, he was unable to eat and continued unwell until the

Boatman with horse, twentieth century.

Monday morning. On that day, an assistant to Mr Sutton, a surgeon of Smethwick, was called in. The boy complained of an injury to his right thigh, and leeches were applied. Then on the recommendation of the assistant surgeon, Goodwin was taken on 27 January to the Queen's Hospital, but never reported that his injuries had been the result of violence.

When called to give evidence about his son, the father, William Goodwin, stated that, on 26 January, he had seen his boy lying on a sofa at his lodgings. He had complained about his knee, and there were twelve leeches on his thigh, which was swollen. When Goodwin asked his son where the scabs on his lip had come from, the boy replied that they had been caused by the boatman with whom he worked, William Parker. He went on to add that Parker had knocked him down and kicked his knee, his back, and once in his belly. This had occurred near a bridge by the James Iron Foundry at the side of the canal near Walsall. The boy explained that Parker had treated him so because he had had an accident with a boat rope and hadn't done his work properly. On concluding his statement, the father could not account for the boy having spoken to Sarah Hadley regarding the rheumatism, for he had never heard of it before.

The next witness was Thomas Spinks, an annealer who lived in Pleck Lane near Walsall. He said that he was employed at the James factory on the morning of 20 January. At four o'clock, he, in company with a youth named Samuel Bird, had heard a cry of 'O good Lord', after which he had watched the deceased walk over to a fence near the Bridgeman Street Bridge. The boy was crying very much. A moment or two later, Spinks saw a man – he could not say whether it was Parker or not – walk toward the deceased and threaten to 'give him some more' if he did not go on. The boy, who was still crying, then walked over to the boat and got in it. As the boat moved away,

Walsall Bottom Lock, close to where the boy John Goodwin was injured.

Spinks shouted to the lad to ask him what the boatman had done to him; the boy replied that he had been kicked by him.

The inquest then moved on to testimony from persons at the Queen's Hospital to discover the final steps leading up to the death of the boy. Doctor Tolly, House Surgeon, stated that the boy had been admitted to the hospital on 27 January. He had a large fluctuated swelling to the right thigh and was also suffering with a fever. The abscess was opened, after which the patient progressed tolerably well for the next three weeks. It was then decided that it was necessary for the leg to be amputated. After the operation, Tolly stated that the boy had rallied for a while but had finally died from pyaemia. Such effects might have occurred spontaneously and might or might not be connected with any previous injuries.

The coroner then summed up the facts. He remarked that there was no legal evidence against anybody. He then asked Parker, who had been present throughout the proceedings, if he had anything to say. Parker was duly cautioned and sworn in. He stated that on Christmas morning at about four o'clock, he and the deceased had been boating toward the Perry Bar Locks, and he had sent the boy on to fill the lock, and while at the lock, the boy had had an accident with the boat horse, after which he said that he was unable to work.

The Inquiry was then adjourned, and unfortunately, I was unable to find any follow up to the story in later editions of the newspaper. Of course, one can only imagine the account and come to one's own conclusions as to what really happened nearly 140 years ago. In the end, the boy died of pyaemia, a type of septicaemia (blood poisoning). Let us hope that Parker truly regretted his part in the boy's demise. In any event, the case certainly gives us something to think about the next time we pass through Walsall or Perry Bar Locks.

Narrow boats waiting to enter Blisworth Tunnel in July 1914. (C. McCutcheon)

Old Tipton, next to the Fountain Inn, with Shropshire Union boat and boat family.

CASE 3
DEATH BY TOWROPE ON THE GRAND UNION:
WILLIAM HICKMAN, INDICTED FOR THE MANSLAUGHTER
OF ANN BRIDGES

When a quarter-of-a-ton horse pulls a 25- to 30-ton boat, enormous strains are created, as anyone can witness by the grooves worn into brickwork at bridge holes or on cast-iron bridge parapets. Towing was never an accident-free occupation, though sometimes the tediousness of the job, especially when working long hours and into the dark, created obvious hazards. On other occasions, irresponsible working or complete foolishness caused accidents. This is a case from the Old Bailey Court in London of a man named Isaac Bridges and his wife Ann, who travelled from Tipton to London to deliver a load of iron and return with a load of wheat. Isaac's brother Alfred was following in a second boat; they both worked for Bissell's of Tipton Green. The boatman spent much of one week walking to London, unloading and loading with a back load, and then spent the next week walking back, to repeat again and again. As a rough guide to distances covered, from Tipton Green Bridge to Paddington Basin, it is 154 miles and 169 locks. A modern cruising guide would calculate this as a nine-day journey, when an average cruising day of eight hours is factored into the equation.

On the return journey, the Bridges encountered many boats heading for London and used what should have been common practice for passing horse boats. Unfortunately, the driver of one boat, a William Hickman, did not follow the passing code, and thus the towrope from his boat swept the deck of Isaac's boat, pulling his wife Ann into the water, and she later died from her ordeal. This is a summary of the court proceedings.

William Hickman is being tried for the manslaughter of Ann Bridges on 22 November 1847. The account is given verbatim; hearing real people answer the questions adds to the impact. The first witness called to the stand was Isaac Bridges.

William Hickman, feloniously killing and slaying Ann Bridges; he was also charged on the Coroner's inquisition with the like offence.

Mr. Huddleston conducted the Prosecution.

Isaac Bridges. I am in the employment of Messrs. Bissell, of Tipton, and am captain of a boat which is used for the conveyance of iron upon the Grand Junction Canal, from Tipton to London. On Friday, 29th Oct., I had a loaded boat on the canal, drawn by one horse, going from London towards Birmingham – when I got near to a place called Dawley-deep, I saw two boats coming in a direction from Birmingham – I was at that time driving my horse – it was about six o'clock in the evening – it was not over dark, it was dusk – my wife was steering the boat – I know the prisoner, but can't say how long he has been on the canal – it is the practice for any boat going from London to Birmingham to keep the road to Branston [boatman's term for Braunston] – the boats coming into London should drop their line and let the other boats swim over their rope – the horse drawing the boats from London should go on the canal side, and the horse drawing the boat towards London should keep the hedge side, drop the line, and let the horse pass over it – the prisoner was with the second of the two boats, which was thirty or forty yards from the first – I passed the first man's boat in the right way, when I met his horse he turned my horse over the line and dropped his rope in the correct way, his horse keeping the hedge side of the towing-path – that was a boat called the *Thistle*.

The prisoner's boat was the *Wellington* – when I met him, his horse was against the water's edge – that was its wrong place – there was not space enough left between his horse and the water's edge for me to drive my horse on the inside – he did not stop his horse – I hove my line over his horse's head, and then my line was in its right place, exactly as if my horse had gone over his line – his line was under mine – if he had stopped then and sunk his line, my boat would have gone over it as it did over the first – he did not stop – I called out to him loud enough for him to hear – I hooted for him to stop his horse, and he did not – the rope by which the boat is drawn is attached to a small mast, which you cannot pull forward, but a little thing will pull it back – that is to enable the rocks to fall off – the prisoner's line loosed mine from the boat, swept the deck, and made fast to my wife who was steering – the line fastened round her wrist and pulled her completely out of the boat into the water – I do not know what became of the prisoner – he did not stop to assist in getting my wife out of the water – my wife died on the next Friday night – her name was Ann Bridges.

Cross-examined by Mr Prendergast. Q. Did you jump into the water?

Isaac. Yes – I did not see the prisoner when I came ashore, not to notice him – my boat was coming from Paddington – I ought to have been on the side nearest the water, instead of which I was on the outside, because there was not room for me on the other – the prisoner knew he was on his wrong side, because he saw me heave the line over the horse's head – his boat was on the right side, but he was on the wrong – I called to him before I met him to put his horse on the right side, and he pulled his horse in to the water's edge – it is a common thing, when two horses meet, for the opposite party to put their horse on the right side – I relied upon his doing that – I was behind my horse, minding my line over the other boat – we are not always at our horse's head – that was not the reason of my being on my wrong side; but he pulled his horse so near the water's edge, that my horse could not get on the right side – my horse was not further from the water than it ought to have been – if I had been at his head I could have put him in a different position, if the prisoner would have let me – I cannot say whether he would or not – it was not owing to my looking after the rope that my horse got wrong – my horse would have been on his right side if the prisoner had kept his horse away – my looking after the rope had nothing to do with it – if he had kept his horse right, mine would have been right. I relied on his keeping his horse right, and I told him to do so – it is a usual thing to say, 'Put your horse on your right side' – I swear that I said so to him – he made no answer – I do not know that I had ever seen him before – I did not know his name, and cannot say that I ever spoke to him – I knew him again when I saw him afterwards – I told him to stop his horse after I hove the line over his horse's head – we do not generally throw the line over, but such jobs are frequently done – it ought not to be done – the usual thing is to put the horses the right way, and then the lines will be right – the lines cross when we meet – that is the signal for the man coming towards London to stop, and let the rope slacken in the water – each boat had one horse – the horse going from London should be nearest the water. I was pulled out of the water by a rope which I caught hold of – it was my brother who pulled me out – people sometimes follow the rule about going to and from London, and sometimes not – many frequently follow it – it is quite as often neglected as followed.

Mr. Huddleston [questioned Isaac regarding passing procedure]. Q. How would the ropes go if a person did not follow that rule?

Isaac. If they do not follow that rule there must be some mischief – they ought to follow it – it is a rule well known among the boatmen – there are public notices of it at every toll-clerk's office – there are very few that do not know it – the notices are printed papers stuck up inside the offices – there was room enough on the hedge side of my horse for the prisoner's horse to have gone.

Alfred Bridges [the next witness to appear]. I am the brother of the last witness, and am captain of the boat *George*, on the Grand Junction Canal. My boat was

Hatton Locks near Warwick. At this point, our Tipton boatman has only walked with his horse 32 miles and fifty-three locks – a sixth of his journey to London.

behind my brother's, and going in the same direction – when we got to Dawley-deep we met the *Thistle* and the *Wellington* – the *Thistle* was the first – she cleared my brother's boat by dropping her line under it – the horse of the *Thistle* took the hedge side of the towing-path – I have been a boatman all my life – I do not know the prisoner – I have seen him on the canal for a few months – the rule on the canal is for the boats that go to London to take the way to Branston – that is on the water side of the towing-path – that rule has been established ever since I can remember, which is twenty-five or twenty-six years. I was not near enough to see on which side of the towing-path the prisoner's horse was when he met my brother, nor did I see the ropes till the woman was in the water – the prisoner was with his horse – he stopped his horse after the woman was in the water – she was entangled in the rope – I and my brother got into the water, and after disengaging her from the rope the prisoner went off with his horse – he waited till we got the woman out – the rope was foul of her till we got her out – I and my brother called out to the prisoner, 'Stop the horse, stop the horse!' – that was after she was in the water – I did not hear my brother call out before that – I was twenty or thirty yards behind – he ought to have stopped, and allowed my brother's horse to go over his rope.

Cross-examined. Q. You know that this rule you speak of is quite as much neglected as it is followed?

Alfred. I do not know; it ought to be followed – the signal for stopping the horse is the meeting of the ropes – the horse going to London ought then to stop, and let the line slacken, for the other to go over it.

William Rayner. I am a surgeon, at Uxbridge. I attended the deceased – the cause of death was mortification, arising from the injury she received from the rope – there was mortification of the arm, and gangrene of the lungs in consequence.

Cross-examined. Q. Did you find quite enough to show that she must have died of that?

Rayner. Yes – there was a deep broad impression round her wrist, showing that a very tight ligature had been round it – the place was not mortal – she died on the Friday following the accident, from a shock to the nervous system, produced by that wound – I could not trace any connection between the shock to the nervous system and the wound – whether she died of fright from being knocked into the water I cannot tell – the mortification extended the whole length of the arm to the shoulder, and reaching to the lungs, death ensued.

Richard Roadknight (police-sergeant) [then took the stand]. I apprehended the prisoner on 31st Oct. – I asked him if he was the man that was driving the horse at the time the woman was injured near Uxbridge – he said he was – I said he must go with me to Uxbridge, as she was not likely to live – he said he knew he was wrong by not stopping the horse, and letting the line under their boat instead of over it.

Cross-examined. Q. What else did he say?

Roadknight. He said after the woman was in the water the husband jumped in, and if it had not been for his throwing the rope they would both have been drowned – he did not say that he did not perceive the rope.

Alfred re-examined. It was I who threw the rope to my brother and his wife when they were in the water – the prisoner was on the spot, about ten or twelve yards off, with his horse.

Mr. Lock [a clerk to the Grand Junction Canal Company was then called to answer questions about the waterway rules]. I produce the Act of Parliament constituting the Company, and also the original by-laws – I have not myself seen copies of those by-laws posted along the line – (The Act empowered the Company to make by-laws, one of which imposed a fine upon any person in charge of any loaded boat passing toward Paddington who should not give way to a loaded boat proceeding in a contrary direction.)

Working boats still gather occasionally at Braunston. By the time our boatman from Tipton arrived here, he would have walked 52 miles and negotiated seventy-nine locks. He would still have another 108 miles and 102 locks to go to get to Limehouse Basin in London.

Isaac re-examined. My boat was loaded with corn – the prisoner's boat was also loaded, I cannot say what with, but I could tell she had a goodish load by her depth in the water.

James Roadknight. I am a clerk on the Grand Junction Canal, stationed at Cowley. I have a printed copy of the by-laws posted up in my office – I have not been to any of the other stations.

Cross-examined. Q. You have never seen the prisoner at your station?

James Roadknight. Not until the accident, to my knowledge.

During the trial, before Mr Justice Coltman, the prisoner was given a good character reference, and after deliberation by the judge, he was declared NOT GUILTY. The account is most interesting for its details of horse-boat operations, cargoes and Boat Companies. It goes without saying that it must have been a terrible ordeal for Isaac and his brother to return home to Tipton without Isaac's wife and working partner.

Due to the fact that the Bridges came from Tipton, and because that place was almost as important for canal transport in the early nineteenth century as Birmingham, I shall now try to describe the development of that industrial town to you.

Few people would refer to modern Tipton as an attractive place. To the casual observer, it is now so thoroughly amalgamated to the Greater Birmingham conurbation, that it is indistinguishable from that entity. However, the area has gone through three distinct phases over the last 300 years and played a pivotal role with the industrial canals of the Midlands. During the Middle Ages, Tipton was a collection of small separated communities that included Tipton Green, Princes End, Toll End, Great Bridge, Ocker Hill, Burnt Tree and Horseley Heath, and was of little importance.

During the seventeenth and eighteenth centuries, in Tipton and its neighbouring towns, coal was increasingly used as a fuel, and the working shafts got deeper and

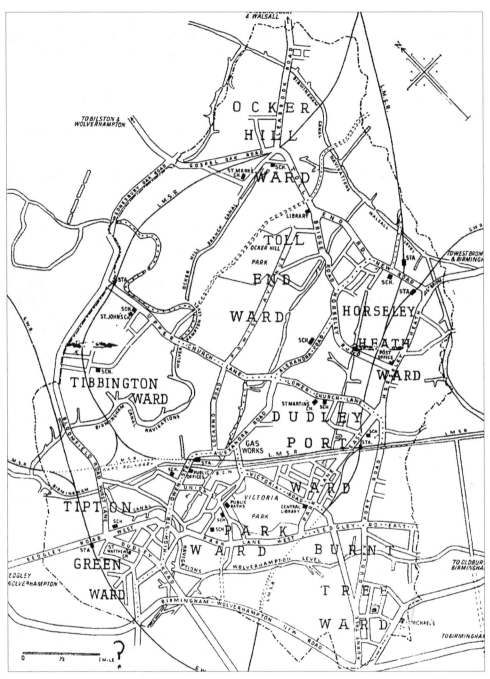

Tipton's canal system showing Tipton Green.

deeper. In 1712, one of the first ever steam engines designed by Newcomen, was erected near Tipton Green to pump out water from a mine. Having said that, some forty years later, Tipton was still a pleasant landscape, described by F. W. Hackwood as having village greens, breezy heathlands, and smiling pastures, intersected by purling streams. It contained pleasant place names such as Lea Brook and Sheepwash, but those rural retreats were soon to vanish, and the culprit was industrial growth and its partner, the Birmingham Canal.

In 1766, the Bill for the Trent & Mersey Canal was presented to Parliament. In the same year, a group of prominent Wolverhampton men who wanted to tie a connection from this enterprise to the Severn – the Staffs & Worcester – got their canal organised. It was totally natural, therefore, that the Birmingham men also wanted to profit from this great inland waterway scheme. After an advertisement was placed in a local newspaper, a meeting was held at the Swan Inn in Birmingham on 28 January the following year. A subscription was taken up in order that James Brindley could carry out a survey. In June, he came with the possibility of two lines that would go from New Hall (Birmingham) to or near Smethwick, Oldbury, Tipton Green, Bilston and from there to a junction with the Staffordshire & Worcestershire Canal.

By July, £35,400 had been subscribed; the act was obtained in the following year, with Brindley being hired for his services at £200 p.a., with the promoters urging a speedy start to the venture. Work was started on the main line toward Tipton with a branch leaving that line in West Bromwich and going another four miles to the mines at Hill Top near Wednesbury. This came to be known as the Wednesbury Canal, though indeed it fell far short of Wednesbury town centre because of the topography. The ten miles from the Birmingham terminus to the Hill Top mines were completed first so that coal could be quickly sold at the city. Tipton was reached by about the same time, and the final through route through to Aldersley Junction on the Staffs & Worcs was finished by 1772. By this time, coal was flooding into Birmingham on the BCN Company's boats at about 300 tons per day.

If you now take a look at the map of the parish of Tipton, you can see how the first Brindley line, now called the Old Main Line, comes into Tipton territory at the top left from Wolverhampton, wriggles its way around Summer Hill, (Tipton's earliest church is at this point) Tibbington and Bloomfield before arriving at Tipton Green. When Brindley was challenged at a later time that the route was inordinately long, he replied that one of the important reasons for the convoluted route was in order that as many of the mines and iron manufactories could be accessed as possible – as we will see later. From Tipton Green, the 28-foot-wide canal with one towpath then wandered toward the base of the Rowley hills and headed for Oldbury. The terminus of the Wednesbury Canal is only just off the top right of the map.

As soon as the Main Line was completed, branches were started to Ocker Hill and later to the Horseley coalmines at Toll End. The Ocker Hill branch was completed by 1774, and this was the start of the criss-crossing of the Tipton Landscape. Before many years had gone by, work was started on the Walsall canal. This started from a junction on the Wednesbury Canal at Ryder's Green, and descended toward Great Bridge by eight locks; it was up and running by 1786. Branches then came off this, and the earlier branch to Toll End was lengthened to join the Walsall. Meanwhile, smaller basins and arms proliferated. Other important connections included the Earl of Dudley's limestone mines at Dudley. He funded a cutting (Lord Wards Canal) from the line at Tipton Green, and took it under the Dudley Hill. Several underground cuttings were dug into the great limestone deposits of this hill, some over 1,000 yards long. Before the end of the eighteenth century, one of these cuts became part of the Dudley tunnel in 1792. Tipton was now at the heart of the BCN operations.

More developments came in the 1820s, when Thomas Telford was employed by the BCN to improve the main line. He initially came upon a canal that he described in his own words as being not much better than a ditch, where boats caused delays from overcrowding and where horses frequently stumbled into the water through the lack of a good towpath. The improvements of this period from 1824 to 1830 saw a much straighter, wider canal with twin towpaths. We now call it the New Main Line, with the Tipton/Dudley Port section being called the Island Line. Telford made these important changes all the way to Birmingham, by either improving the line or cutting across the loops. At the left of the map, you can see where he shortened the route by cutting off the Summer Hill section by taking it through the later Coseley Tunnel. The very last great additions to the Tipton network came in the 1840s with the Tame Valley Canal, and the Netherton Tunnel of 1858.

This brings me nicely to the calculating part, and I am always ready to be corrected if necessary. However, I believe that the relatively small area of Tipton had, by the middle of the nineteenth century, more miles of industrial canal per square mile than any other parish in the country. Within its misshapen 3 miles by 2, that is to say, approximately 5 square miles, there were 13½ miles of man-made waterway, composed of 4¼ miles of Old Main Line, 2 miles of New Main Line, 1¼ miles of the Walsall canal, plus 6 miles of branches. And that's not counting many smaller basins.

With the three vital ingredients of minerals, steam power and an efficient transport system all established, a massive industrial expansion took place not only in Tipton but the surrounding Black Country. To supply the manpower for this increase, workers and their families flocked in from Wales, Ireland, Shropshire, Gloucester, and Somerset. In 1801, twenty-five years after the establishment of the Birmingham Canal, there were 4,288 people residing in the parish. Only fifty years later, there were 24,853, an increase of 500 per cent. In 1798, there were only 800 houses in the parish, mostly inhabited by the poor; by 1851, there were 4,705 occupied houses, with twenty-three being constructed. Not surprisingly, coal was removed in ever-greater quantities, and iron production increased with it. The majority of iron production during the eighteenth century had centred around the River Severn, but after the arrival of the Birmingham Canal network, South Staffordshire furnaces grew in number and output, so that by 1823, they had overtaken their Shropshire rivals.

The Horseley Company was to become typical of this growth. In 1792, the Horseley estate was purchased by Joseph Amphlett, Edward Dixon and William Bedford (who also happened to be solicitor for the BCN), and a branch from Tipton Green was cut with three locks. The site was quickly developed for coal extraction. The company, not long after this, entered into the iron trade – the two were inseparable – and went on to produce some of the most wonderful iron bridges for the canal system. There are several to be found around the BCN, i.e., at Bromford and Smethwick Junctions, with probably the Galton Bridge over the Smethwick cutting being the most famous – and the largest of its time. There continued a great relationship between the coal works, the iron trade and the canal, as other examples will testify. Iron masters developed their concerns at the edge of the canal and came to include, amongst many more, Tipton Green Furnaces, The Toll End Iron Works, who also made bridges for the canals on the Netherton Branch, Gospel Oak and Summer Hill Iron Works, and John Bagnall & Sons in Great Bridge.

The iron trade started off in Tipton with small products, often labelled 'toys', as it did in many other Black Country towns. And then, as the capacity of the blast furnaces grew ever greater, larger products began to be made. Some companies like James Fisher and James Bate manufactured hinges – the latter employed about 100 hands. However, in the early days, the nail trade employed many people – about one quarter of the workforce. This trade, based often in a crude outbuilding attached to a poor-quality house was the workplace for a whole family, where children started as

Bomb damage at Tipton during the First World War. (K. Hodgkins)

soon as they were big enough to wield a hammer. The different kinds of nails were numerous, from 2-ounce tack nails, which work out at 1,200 nails to equal 2 ounces, up to large spikes. Every nail was formed individually from iron strip. Considerable quantities of horse nails were likewise made. The competition in this basic trade was always high, which caused many to be thrown out of work because of not meeting adequate standards. This applied particularly to children and old people.

At the beginning of the nineteenth century, when the country was involved in its great struggle against Napoleon, the situation in Tipton and the surrounding towns was especially tough, leading to unrest and the bread riots. On Monday 28 April 1800, a Dudley mob sought to enlist the Tipton colliers on their side in an attack on the baker's shops. They were at first dissuaded by Mr Amphlett, a local magistrate (and Horseley Company). Later in the afternoon, they made their way over to the nine locks in Brierley Hill, where they took possession of two canal boats laden with grain and heading for Birmingham. When the Dudley Volunteer Cavalry made an appearance, they were attacked with bricks, stones and bulldogs. Then the riot act was read while the Infantry Association and regular dragoons came to assist. The riot came to a conclusion only after one rioter had been killed and many wounded. Riots continued in other Black Country locations.

Work in any of the industries at this time was a dangerous affair, and perhaps the most dangerous of all was mining the coal seams. In 1849, there was a particularly tragic accident at the 'Blue Fly Pit' in Dudley Port where sixteen men and boys lost their lives. In 1851, a large piece of coal was sent from Tipton to the Great Exhibition in London. After being raised from the Denbigh Colliery at a depth of 495 feet, and weighing a massive 13 tons, it was cut by Round's Colliery at Tividale, into a smooth silver cylinder weighing six tons. It was polished until it resembled jet. I think that this case alone demonstrates the importance of coal and also the pride of its extractors in that mineral.

Modern Tipton Green; the building on the left is the old Round's Wharf Building, originally built *c.* 1800, one of the very few buildings that the Bridges family would recognise.

In addition to coalmining and the making of iron, Tipton developed its heavy engineering trades, which include the production of castings, forgings, structural ironwork, steam engines, boilers, chains and anchors. In 1825, the Horseley Iron Works built the world's first iron steam ship and, in 1829, Telford's Galton Bridge. In 1843, the Gospel Oak Ironworks made the cast-iron columns for the Albert Dock in Liverpool, which are now part of a listed building. In 1856, the firm of H. P. Parkes built the world's then largest anchor for Brunel's steamship the *Great Eastern*. It is not surprising that Tipton was described by the well-known Midland historian F. W. Packwood as 'palpitating with the beat and throb of a thousand engines'.

Many different kinds of boats plied the Tipton Canals. In addition to the slow plod of single-class goods (i.e., loaded with one commodity, such as coal) there were fly-boats that travelled at a good trot, and horses were changed at regular intervals, just as post horses in a chaise journey. Those fly-boats were all timed at regular intervals along the route, just as buses and trains are today, and their hulls were designed to pass through the water much more efficiently. Also, there were the packet boats, designed and scheduled to carry passengers only. In 1851, Swift Packets run by Thomas Monk of Tipton were carrying passengers from Wolverhampton to Birmingham via Tipton in 2 hours 10 minutes for 1s. The now-famous firm of Fellows, Morton & Clayton had its beginnings in 1837 next door to Tipton, in West Bromwich by James Fellows. He started to concentrate on the long-distant trade and, by 1855, was taking as much as 13,000 tons of iron from the Birmingham area down to London. As the business continued to grow, he moved his base of operations to Toll End in Tipton, then describing himself as a canal and railway carrier.

Wharves abounded as at Tipton Green for the transfer of goods, but none was larger than what came to be called Dudley's Port. Dudley is, of course, right next to Tipton but could never be served with a direct canal because it sits on a hill. But Dudley's traffic was never neglected, because warehouses and an extensive horse-drawn tram system were established to cater for Dudley's needs. At least seven tramlines, one of those alone having ten termini, carried coal to the boats, while other goods from all over the country were unloaded from the boats and transhipped either onto the rail system or onto carts to be taken to Dudley. FMC came to have a warehouse at Dudley Port.

At Tipton Green, carriers who developed this early integrated transport system were the local firms of Bissell and Whitehouse, along with the better-known carrier of Pickford's & Co. and Crowley & Co. A directory of 1835 gives us a good picture of the busy canal traffic from Tipton thus:

To London, Liverpool, Manchester, Birmingham and all parts of the Kingdom, fly boats from Pickford's and Co., Crowley & Company's wharf, Tipton Green, daily.

To London, Liverpool, Manchester, Bristol, Worcester, Birmingham, Shrewsbury, fly boats from John Whitehouse and Sons wharf, Tipton Green, every day.

To London, Liverpool, Manchester, Shardlow, Hull and Gainsborough, from Job Bissell's wharf, Tipton Green, three times a week.

To London, Liverpool, Manchester, Worcester &c from Tildasley and Sturlands wharf, Tipton Green, three times a week.

Ocker Hill engine-room, early twentieth century. (K. Hodgkins)

To Birmingham in two hours, Thomas Monk's packet for goods and passengers from the Bush Factory Bridge, and Fountain Inn Owen Street, Tuesday, Thursday and Saturday morning at half-past 8, return same evening.

Water supplies were of first consideration in the planning stage of the Birmingham Canal. The Wolverhampton section came to be built on the 473-foot level, while the rest of the section to Birmingham came to be 20 feet lower on the 453-foot level (actually, until the end of the eighteenth century, there was an even higher level between the locks at Smethwick, but this was lost with Smeaton's improvements). To supply water, the canal therefore had two reservoirs built, one at Smethwick, with a second at Titford near Oldbury. As the network expanded, i.e., to Walsall, Worcester and Fazeley, much more water was lost down the sets of locks leading to those destinations. To cope with this loss, the BCN Company started to purchase steam engines from James Watt and Matthew Boulton, and one of the first came to be built at the Spon Lane locks in West Bromwich. The Ocker Hill branch was also susceptible to water loss and, in 1784, received its own pumping engine and pumped up water from the much lower Walsall Canal, which happened to be only a few hundred yards away. A tunnel was built from the Walsall branch and under the Ocker Hill terminus. This was the start of the development of the Ocker Hill Pumping Station and Maintenance Yard. More engines came to be added to the BCN system as a whole, but nowhere had as many as the Ocker Hill branch. This yard, which started life as a coal wharf and limekilns, came to be the hub of operations on the BCN system. Many men came to be employed here as stokers for the large Lancashire-style boilers, as boat builders and repairers, or to manufacture lock gates and anything out of wood or iron for the canal's infrastructure. By the early twentieth century, the old styles of beam engines were outdated and were replaced by much more efficient triple-expansion steam engines manufactured by Hathorn Davey. To illustrate the work that was going on at this station, in one year alone, the operational costs for pumping work was £11,000. The yard closed in 1959.

No piece on Tipton would be complete without a mention of its two famous canal characters, the Tipton Slasher, whose life appears in my other book, *Tales from the West Midland Canals*, and Caggy Stevens. The Tipton Slasher, real name William Perry, was the bare-knuckle boxing champion in England between 1850 and 1857, and the 'Slasher' part of the title refers to the style of swing that he used while boxing. Perry started out life working the Tipton canals by boating away the 'night soil' as it was euphemistically called. He is reputed to have done his fighting apprenticeship at the local locks – it wasn't uncommon for men to fight for the right to go through a lock. Born in 1820, he was a lad when Telford made the Main Line improvements mentioned earlier. After a promising, pugilistic start, he made a reputation and a lot of money by fighting a variety of contenders. Unfortunately, not a good businessman, he lost his last fight and his money, and ended up pretty much where he began. Alan Stevens, on the other hand, nicknamed 'Caggy', became a horse boater about 100 years after the Slasher. And although he saw the decline of the canal throughout the 1950s and 1960s, Caggy always managed to find a little niche by where he could carry on his small operation of horse boating. Occasionally working with an assistant, Caggy did some coal transport, rubbish removal or canal maintenance work and managed to carry on the horse-boating tradition right up to about 1980.

As mentioned at the outset, it is difficult for a resident of today's Tipton to imagine what the town was like just 100 years ago. Modern society has swept away most of the symbols of the canal-based industrial world, as well as the back-to-back dwellings that folk lived in. Now only the fine exhibits at the Black Country Living Museum, found on the border of Tipton and Dudley, can give a flavour of those earlier years. Indeed, Tipton is a town whose contribution to the industrial world and the world of the Birmingham Canal Network should never be forgotten.

CHAPTER 5

Manslaughter – Child Cruelty

Before Mr Baron Amphlett. December 8th 1875.
Murder of Elizabeth Lowke at Aldersley Junction.

In December 1875, a boatman, Frederick Musson, and his female assistant Anna Maria Hillman, were brought before the Stafford County Assizes for the wilful murder of a small child, Elizabeth Lowke, aged seven, in the previous October. The incident happened at Aldersley on the Staffordshire & Worcestershire Canal

Aldersley was the first important junction of the BCN with the Staffordshire & Worcestershire Canal in 1772. It is situated at the bottom of the Wolverhampton 21 Locks, about a mile and a half from the centre of that bustling town. From that date onward, boats could access a wider world, and this importance continued until the Birmingham & Fazeley Canal opened in 1789. Later on in 1815, the Birmingham & Worcester Canal opened, thus granting another way out from the BCN to the south. Obviously, as each exit in turn opened, it lessened the traffic at the original gateway, but there was always a high volume of traffic going through Aldersley to maintain its status. As a consequence, both the Staffs & Worcs and the BCN Company built important offices right at the connection of the two waterways.

Our photographs from the 1950s depict Aldersley much as it would have appeared at the time of the crime. Notice that at that time there was a delightful little archway for the horses travelling on the opposite towpath. The four-storey building was called Autherly House, and it was built in 1773-74. Connected to it were two semi-detached buildings known as Oxley Moor buildings. Today, of course, as our more recent photographs show, all the buildings have gone, but at least the lower parts of the structure have been tastefully left to give a kind of porthole into the past.

Right until the middle of the twentieth century, Aldersley was an exceedingly busy junction, with as many as 20,000 boats per year coming through the bottom lock of the Wolverhampton 21 alone. A fixed community of canal company workers with their wives and children lived at the junction from year to year, while with every passing day, a community in flux comprising passing boatmen and their families made up a secondary part of Aldersley's world. Interestingly, the junction has never had a road connection, and that is why there is a noticeably secluded feel to the place, even though the heart of Wolverhampton is only a short distance away.

On 30 October 1875, a horse boat operated by a young man and woman arrived at Aldersley in the late hours and tied up. Frederick Musson immediately unhitched the horse and took it along to the stables, where he brushed the animal down and made sure that it had water and feed. It had worked hard that day and was in need of a rest.

Aldersley Junction looking north, mid-twentieth century.

Aldersley Junction looking south along the Staffordshire & Worcestershire Canal.

Aldersley today.

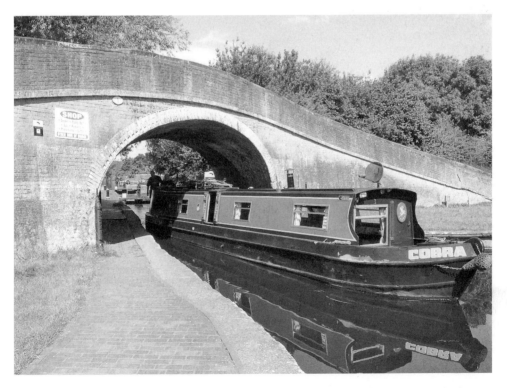

Autherley Junction of the Staffs & Worcestershire Canal and the Shropshire Union Canal of 1835.

Meanwhile, his partner, but certainly not his wife, placed coal on the range and commenced cooking a late dinner. Like a dozen others that night, they would make Aldersley their home. Fifty feet away was a boat worked by the Mander family; they would constitute some of the witnesses to the demise of the young girl.

Some months earlier a Mr Lowke, who already had several of his children on his boat, had asked the pair to take his daughter Elizabeth in order to ease the burden of his overpopulated craft. He trusted that they would look after his daughter; he was to be sadly mistaken in this.

Frederick Musson was uneducated, and of a brutish nature, his partner Anna Hillman could have exhibited the more delicate and motherly qualities of her sex, but unfortunately she did not. For some time, the pair had been treating the seven-year-old girl with great harshness; she had latterly become emaciated and sickly in appearance. On 30 October, when the prisoners' boat was passing Aldersley Junction, the deceased was seen sitting on the footboard of the boat, her only clothing being a skirt which did not go all the way around her. As soon as Musson had eaten, he muttered a few words of contempt to the child and headed for the nearest pub. After drinking, his attitude was often worse than before.

That evening, the girl was left alone in the boat for some time. Between seven and eight o'clock, the female, Hillman, returned to the boat accompanied by Tom Mander from a neighbouring boat. Mander noticed straight away that there was a disagreeable smell in the boat, and Hillman at once accused the little girl of having caused it, and complained of her dirty habits. She then took a whip and beat the child while it lay on the floor clothed only in a shift. Then taking the deceased by the hair, she pulled her up from the floor. The whole thing distressed Tom, and he told Hillman not to hurt the poor

Boat gathering in 2008 near Aldersley.

Wolverhampton Locks looking toward Aldersley Junction.

little thing, for she might not do it again – to which Hillman replied, 'The little — was always doing it.' She then took off the child's chemise and it got upon the side bed out of the way. It was then naked with the exception of its boots and stockings. Subsequently, when Tom left the boat and returned to his father's boat, they all heard a child crying.

Mary Mander, Tom's mother, then walked along to Hillman's boat to see what she could do. Mrs Mander appealed to Hillman, as her son had done before her, not to abuse the child anymore, and Hillman did promise not to beat the child anymore, but she did say that if Fred (Musson) knew what the child had done, he would have probably done worse. Hillman told Mary Mander that, more than once, Fred had threatened to kill the child or simply throw her into the cut. Mary advised Hillman to wipe the child clean and put it to bed, and say nothing to Fred of what had taken place.

When Musson returned to his boat later that night, the drink was in, and his wits were out. He was ready to take his frustrations out on a small, defenceless girl. On entering the tiny cabin, he hit her hard with the stock of his whip, and promptly went to sleep. The next morning, when he and Hillman awoke, they were confronted by the cold corpse of the girl. Musson was at a loss what to do; Hillman replied that the deed could not be covered up and encouraged Musson to go and seek one of the officials at the company offices only a hundred yards away.

The first person he met was Charles Millington, a clerk at Aldersley Junction. Musson asked Millington to go to his boat; he claimed that the child he had with him had had a fit or fainted away. As they walked along the towpath, Musson explained to Millington that he and his partner had prepared to get going that morning but discovered the child dead. When the clerk entered the cabin, he put his hand on the child and felt that it was cold. He noticed that the right eye was very discoloured and asked Musson and Hillman how they accounted for that? And they both said that the child had fallen in the cabin. Millington then said that they must go for a doctor and a policeman, and Musson went in search of both. In about an hour and a half, he came back, and said he had seen a policeman.

Later, Millington and Police Constable Clayton went along to the boat and went down into the cabin; Millington noticed that the face of the child had been washed in his absence. When Constable Clayton and Police Sergeant Billet inquired as to how the girl came to be covered in bruises, the couple replied that she had been trodden on by the horse. Police Inspector Hackney later deposed to searching the prisoners' boat, and finding an apron stained with blood.

At the trial, Mr John Cook, Surgeon of Tettenhall, stated that he had made an examination of the body. It was very much emaciated and there were cuts and bruises all over it. He described the character of the injuries in detail. He was of the opinion that the injuries had been produced by blows; undoubtedly many of them had been caused by the lash of a whip, and others were such as the stock of a whip would have inflicted. Having regard to the various wounds and bruises he found, he was of the opinion they could not have been caused by the tread of a horse. Internally, the organs were all healthy, and he found that the cause of death was a layer of coagulated blood upon the brain. There were indications of repeated blows about the head, and he was of the opinion that the clot of blood upon the brain had been produced by a blow or blows to the temple; administered certainly within twenty-four hours – it might be within a few hours of death. The clot of blood would produce a coma, which would continue until death.

Mr Underhill then summed up the case for the prosecution, and directed the attention of the jury to the law upon murder and manslaughter. He recounted the history of the child from the time it was delivered by its father into the hands of the prisoners. He did not wish to put it that she was a strong and robust child, but there could be no doubt generally she was a healthy child, but if in some respects she was a weakling, that was a circumstance which ought to have appealed to the tender mercies of the prisoners.

Mooring at Aldersley.

Coming to the night when the child was last seen alive, the learned counsel said the jury could not penetrate the cabin of the boat and see what was there enacted, but they could draw a conclusion from the surrounding circumstances. They would bear in mind that, on a former occasion, the prisoner Musson was seen to strike the child on the head with a whip stock, and the evidence from the doctor that death had probably resulted from repeated blows from such an instrument. They had the fact that the child was beaten late at night for a particular act by the female prisoner in the absence of Musson and that subsequently cries were heard proceeding from the boat about the time when Musson was known to have returned to it. The next morning, the child was dead. The jury would have to consider whether in the cabin that night something took place that was the immediate cause of the death of the child.

Mr Plowden then addressed the jury for the defence. He argued that the acts proved against the prisoners were not sufficient to justify the jury in finding them guilty of murder, because they did not form a sufficiently strong foundation on which to build the theory that they were accountable for the condition in which the body was found after death. He summarised the evidence to show the nature and extent of the actual violence towards the child that had been proved against the prisoners and pointed out that, in every instance in which violence had been used, the child had been guilty of some act which had irritated the prisoners, no case of utterly meaningless and wanton cruelty having been proved against them. The jury must take into consideration the fact that an ignorant man like Musson, seeing an act continually repeated, would think that he had to deal with an obstinate child persisting in filthy habits in spite of all he could do to eradicate them. Generally, the counsel contended, all that had been proved against the prisoners was that they had acted upon different occasions with a mistaken idea of punishment.

The learned judge having summed up the case and having pointed out the different bearings of the evidence.

The jury retired, and after an absence of thirty minutes, they returned into court and delivered a verdict of manslaughter against both prisoners. The foreman stated that the jury wished to give expression to their unanimous opinion that the father of the deceased was deserving of censure for his parental neglect of duty.

As the case approached its termination, the prisoners appeared to be much affected by their position, their agitation finding relief in tears, but they were calm while awaiting the verdict. When the jury returned into court, Musson appeared to await the announcement of the verdict with intense eagerness, and it was evident that he experienced immense relief on being pronounced not guilty of murder. The woman was more stolid in her appearance at this juncture.

His Lordship then pronounced sentence in these terms: 'Frederick Musson and Anna Maria Hillman – after very careful enquiry, the jury have, I have no doubt after very anxious consideration, found it in their power to return a verdict of manslaughter only. Your offence as nearly approaches to murder as can be, and I do not hesitate to say that if the jury had taken a different view of the offence and found you guilty of murder, I should, as far as I have any influence on the question, have left you both for execution. I do not mean to say the jury are wrong in their conclusion, on the contrary; I think I should have done the same thing in their place; but considering the enormity of your conduct towards this child, and having not the slightest doubt your action did cause the death of the child – to which at least one of you had promised to be kind – I must pass a most severe sentence against you, not only as a punishment for this offence, but as a warning to other people who undertake a charge of this kind.

'The sentence of the court is that each of you be kept in penal servitude for twenty years.'

CHAPTER 6

The Rape and Murder of Christina Collins on the Trent & Mersey Canal, First Trial

THE MURDER OF CHRISTINA COLLINS ON THE TRENT AND MERSEY CANAL JUNE, 1839 by THREE of PICKFORD'S BOATMEN

Or, as it was titled in *The Stafford Advertiser*, 1839:

ALLEGED VIOLATION AND MURDER OF A FEMALE ON THE CANAL BY BOATMEN

This case is a most fascinating one, as it appears in two parts. The first trial takes place in 1839, and the second a year later. At the end of the first trial, the three prisoners are declared Not Guilty, and it appears that they are ready to walk free, when an unusual event occurs: a witness appears who claims to have new evidence against the men. However, this new witness is one Joseph Orgill, who was incarcerated at the same time with James Owen, the captain of the boat, and one of the main perpetrators. Orgill tells the authorities that while imprisoned with Owen, the latter not only secretly confessed the crime to his cellmate, but gave details of the rape. Orgill is given a pardon to enable him to give evidence at the later trial of Owen, Thomas and Ellis. There is then the second trial, when the very same witnesses are produced, and in effect the prisoners are tried for the same offence after initially having been acquitted, which is a rare thing in British courts.

And then, when the final damning verdict is released – death for all three prisoners – a gentleman rushes away to London by train to frantically seek a pardon for Ellis. William Ellis is one of the three men on trial, but it appears that several of the men of law are convinced that he had nothing to do with the murder and rape of the woman. Is he hanged or freed? You will find out for yourself.

Also, this case highlights the fact that night working was a regular part of boating life in the nineteenth century. Imagine for a moment that you have just completed a full day's cruising, including the passage of some ten to twenty locks. Now imagine having done that, and more at night. Impossible, you may say, undoubtedly dangerous, you add, but night working was common practice throughout much of the canal age, and that with a horse to drive under bridges and around bends, with zero lighting. There was the captain in the hatches, steering by the glint of light on the water's surface and perhaps a dull oil lantern at the fore end. A full moon may have given a little illumination but only on a clear night.

As more and more canals were built in the final quarter of the eighteenth century, more boats were added to a growing system, and greater distances were covered. Just

Tixall Lock, Staffordshire & Worcestershire Canal, showing how arches were painted white to assist night working.

as an example of how traffic was growing, in 1793, 100 boats were seen to pass over the Birmingham Canal summit. Thirty years later, Josiah Baxendale, on his periodic inspection of Pickford's stations, passed upwards of 400 empty or loaded boats in the same area. With a rapidly expanding economy, the pressures of trade made sure that more boats, with a faster and more reliable service should evolve, and large companies employing many hundreds of men and boys came to the fore. Pickford's and Bache's were of that number.

In the beginning, bulk conveyance of such goods as coal and iron was common, but with an efficient service, perishables and even passengers were transported from city to city.

THE FLY-BOAT SYSTEM

The so-called fly-boat, that is to say, a boat that travelled both day and night with only short stops, was the solution that these two firms and others used for the conveyance of high-value goods and passengers. Every section of the journey was well timed, in order that merchants and passengers would know exactly when a boat would arrive at its intended destination.

In 1795, Matthew Pickford registered ten such vessels, but by 1832, his fleet had grown to nearly 100 narrow boats. The fly-boat started at fixed times, usually carried no more than 15 tons, and proceeded with all speed both night and day. To accomplish this feat, horses were changed at regular intervals, and a crew of four was required. This usually comprised four males with at least one boy, and they worked a shift pattern. One man steered, one drove the horse, while the other two slept in the small cabin at the rear. If any passengers were accommodated, they probably had a makeshift cabin somewhere near the middle of the boat, though there were few comforts, and the traveller may well have had only a bed of straw.

From the start, canal companies were not happy for boats to be operating throughout the night, because they were loath to miss out on tolls, and were also not keen to have to employ their own men throughout the hours of darkness. In 1799, the Birmingham Company decided that Messrs Bache & Co. stage boats between London and Manchester were to be permitted to pass the stop at Fazeley without interruption, as would the boats of Messrs Pickford & Co. And then over the ensuing decades, as the number of boats increased, the canal company's resistance to this trade was progressively overthrown.

A complex system of fly-boat services thus emerged and reached a developed state by the middle of the nineteenth century, providing rapid lines of transit for exported and imported goods between the interior and various ports. The most important route of all was that between Birmingham and London, and in 1832, some twenty-five fly-boats started out from both locations. The non-stop journey from Birmingham to London took three days and nights, and this included Sunday working.

Some reports state the captains of these non-stop boats were paid well, but when one takes into consideration that they were tied to the boat, as we say these days, 24/7, and they had to pay the other hands from this money, it is obvious that the job only appealed to a few. Pickford's captains seemed to have received a little more than others and, in the first half of the nineteenth century, were being paid 5 guineas for a voyage from Manchester to London, the horses were provided by the company. Regular stations along the route provided a change of horse and fodder, whilst clerks kept a note of the cargoes and progress made. Gauging being undertaken by the relevant canal company.

The following case demonstrates clearly the regular night operations, where several of Pickford's and Bache's boats, and indeed others, are found working well past midnight, and how their crews and fixed operatives such as clerks at the company's stations operated.

This account thus provides a small window into the operations of the fly-boats of the nineteenth century, but the admissions of one of those men also grants a glimpse into another side of their life, and that was a general life of crime. George Thomas of Wombourne admitted just before he was hanged that, amongst boatmen, thieving was an accomplishment, and those men are most sought after by boat captains.

Pickford's were involved with the transport of goods well before the advent of the canals. Early in the eighteenth century, Matthew and Thomas Pickford had a well-developed sytem of fly waggons that used change-over teams of horses and drivers, operating a four-day journey from Manchester to London. As soon as the canals were opened, the company realised that this new technology was going to be good for their business. They entered canal transport in the 1780s with a number of narrow boats. In 1790, a writer commented on the flow of goods by canal from the north of England to Coventry, 'from whence they are taken to London by Mr Pickford's wagons, who has large warehouses on the wharf to store goods.' We also know that in 1794 Pickford's boats were departing daily from Castle Quay for Coventry. By 1817, they had important depots that included, amongst others, Coventry, Derby, Leicester, Birmingham, Blisworth, Braunston, Macclesfield, Stoke Bruerne and Warwick, besides numerous other stations dotted at strategic points along the way – as can be seen in our account regarding the murder of Christina Collins.

Immediately, they took advantage of the Trent & Mersey Canal, bringing goods as far south as Shardlow, but built a base at Rugeley when the Coventry and Oxford

Canals were being constructed. Their aim was always to obtain a constant traffic from the northern cities to the capital and vice versa. When the Grand Junction Canal was being built, Pickford's starting using it straight away, though they did have to tranship to waggons, and back to boats again at Blisworth tunnel until it was completed. Pickford & Co. gave regular public notices regarding their haulage details, and I quote from one of them here, which certainly provides an interesting and useful snapshot into the variety of goods that they dealt with.

PICKFORD & Co
GIVE PUBLIC NOTICE

That they will not be accountable for any article, unless it be entered and signed for as received by them or their agents.

Nor will they be responsible for the loss of or damage to, Money in cash, or Bills, or Promissory Notes, or securities for money, or Jewelry, Bullion, Plate, Clocks, Watches, Trinkets, Rings, Marbles, Lace, Furs, Writings, Prints, Paintings, or other valuables; nor for damage done to China, Glass, Wearing apparel, Musical instruments, Furniture, Toys or any other such hazardous or brittle articles, in packages or otherwise, unless the same be insured according to their value, and paid for at the time of delivery.

Every attention will be paid to the forwarding of such goods as are delivered to PICKFORD and Co, and in the event of their being prevented or delayed in forwarding the same by water, through a stoppage on the canals, from frost, or from breakage of the banks, or from any other cause, such goods as may be required, will be forwarded by land, charging a Land Rate thereon.

JJ Metcalf Printer

In an article in *Waterways World* in 2008, researcher Margaret Beardsmore wrote,

By the 1820s, Pickford's was once more a force to be reckoned with (they had gone through some financial difficulties); the headquarters were moved to City Basin in London, and the run-down boat fleet was gradually replaced and refurbished. The wharf surrounded the southern end of City Basin, with the eastern side being filled with stable blocks. In the middle, the goods warehouse, which provided shelter from the elements, had open sides to transfer cargo quickly between boats and horse waggons. Counting houses and offices took up the whole left-hand side of the basin. There were over one hundred clerks employed, with a huge map on the wall showing the 97 towns where Pickford's had their sub offices to where goods were dispatched.

Harry Hanson came to some interesting conclusions about the boatman in his book of 1975, when he wrote,

The canal age saw the number of canals, boats and boatmen greatly increased. Boats travelled faster and further, and boatmen were called upon to work more arduously. Many of the captains were not of the best character, and that a large number of hands were young men and boys, and that far from the moderating influence of home and community, mischief could result. This was particularly true of the fly-boatmen who had to snatch their pleasures as quickly and intensely as they could. The arrival of wives and families on board slow boats, usually as a substitute for the hired hands, meant that the creation of a rootless separate society was assured.

There has been much speculation about the original boatmen having drifted into their work from having been the hardened navvies that built the cut in the first place. That would certainly explain something of the reputation mentioned in Hanson's book, but this has never been conclusively proven.

Certainly, in the latter half of the nineteenth century, and well into the twentieth, families had come onto the boats. A whole community developed, often unseen and unheard by those without a direct connection. As soon as they were able, children learnt the skills required to work boats from their parents, growing up to then take over their own boats. Snatched moments of courtship at loading or discharge points, or at pubs and other overnight stopping places, often led to courtship and then marriage between members of different families.

However, although the boating community still worked long and hard hours, the days of fly-boating had long gone. By the beginning of the twentieth century, the insular community once seen and branded by many as 'water gypsies' was fast disappearing. Traffic generally on the waterways declined as first railways, and then the roads, took over freight carriage – the end of regular commercial carrying was nigh, and many could see the writing on the wall, though a handful of company's hung on until the bitter end. During these difficult years, men often sought jobs with better hours, pay, and conditions, and so they inevitably moved off the boats with their families and bought, or rented, a house 'on the bank'. Nowadays, it seems easy, without real knowledge of what life was truly like in the nineteenth century, to view the ordinary boat families' existence with the historic sentimentality of rose-tinted glasses, because certainly their lives were tough. Nevertheless, their lives could never have been as hard, rough and unsavoury as those 'ne'er-do-wells' working on the night shift.

THE TRIAL BEGINS

At this point we imagine the interior of the courtroom at Stafford, as the legal teams, Judge and excited spectators take their seats. There is a smell of polished wood, the rustle of legal papers and a murmuring of many voices before a general hush settles over the room. The three prisoners are brought into court by prison guards.

James Owen (39), **George Thomas alias Dobell** (27), and **William Ellis alias Lambert**, (28) were then placed at the bar. There were four indictments against them. The first charged them with the wilful murder of Christina Collins, by throwing her into the canal. (By the Coroner's inquisition they were likewise charged with the same murder.) By the second indictment they were charged with a rape upon the same Christina Collins; different counts charging the different prisoners with being principles in the commission of the offence, and the others as aiders and abettors. Another indictment charged them with a common assault. And a fourth with stealing certain articles, the property of the husband of the unfortunate woman.

The prisoners pleaded not guilty to all the charges. Musson – the boy, who was originally charged with them was not named in the indictment; and it was understood that he would appear as a witness for the crown.

Mr Sergeant Ludlow and Mr F. V. Lee appeared for the prosecution. Mr Godson appeared as counsel for Owen; Mr Yardley for Thomas; and Mr Beadon for Ellis.

Mr Sergeant Ludlow said he should first proceed on the charge of rape; and it was his intention not to offer any evidence against Owen, whom he was willing to admit as a witness for the crown.

Mr Godson said that that was done without Owen's consent.

Mr Yardley and Mr Beadon contended that this was a most extraordinary proceeding, and very unfair toward the prisoners whom they defended; for this would be evidence for which they were altogether unprepared.

Mr Godson understood that this course was being taken by means of a threat held out to Owen.

Mr Sergeant Ludlow thought that Mr Godson's observation was uncalled for and improper. If the counsel for the prosecution in their discretion, considered that it would further the ends of the justice to admit an accused party as a witness, they had a perfect right to do so.

Mr Justice Williams said he did not feel much difficulty on this point; but as the case was one of extreme importance, he should take the opinion of his learned brother, Mr Baron Alderson on the subject. His Lordship then left the court, and on his return stated that, as he before observed, there was very little doubt as to the proper course to be taken in this case. He had known instances, not once, but nearer one hundred times wherein the court had allowed counsel for prosecution to withhold evidence on behalf of the crown. He looked upon it to be a matter of course; and he would leave it to the discretion of the learned counsel to do that which he thought would best promote the interests of public justice in this case.

Mr Sergeant Ludlow then proceeded to open the case, which he described as one of the highest importance, as it concerned the life or death of the prisoners. For the purpose of assisting the jury in a proper understanding of the case he would give a brief general outline of the facts which would be stated in evidence.

The unfortunate woman, Christina Collins, into the particulars of whose treatment and death they had to inquire, was a married woman. She had been obtaining her livelihood for some time as a seamstress in Liverpool. Her husband had left her in Liverpool to obtain employment in London; and she, a short time before this unhappy occurrence, started from Liverpool in order to go to London to join her husband. In the early part of June, her husband wrote her a letter, enclosing a sovereign, and desiring her to come. On Saturday morning the 15th of June, having packed up her clothes, she took her place in one of Pickford and Company boats, leaving Liverpool that morning in a barge for Preston Brook. At that place she entered as a passenger the canal boat of which James Owen was the Captain, and on board of which the two other prisoners, Thomas and Ellis were employed to assist in navigating her. A boy of the name Musson was likewise employed as a hand in the management of that boat. It would be shown by the evidence, that on the voyage, the deceased appeared on several occasions to apprehend some violence from the three men; and at one place she was observed to sharpen a knife; for which act it was not for him – Mr Sergeant Ludlow – to offer a reason: though he believed that one of the prisoners had a scar on his face, and extraordinarily enough, that knife was found in the interior of one of the deceased's trunks, which must have been uncorded and opened, or it would not have found its way thither. He should be able to prove not only apprehension and alarm on the part of the deceased, but also coarse and violent and threatening language on the part of the prisoners: and at one particular place he should show that persons were alarmed by screams proceeding from the woman. The boat ought to have arrived at Fazeley at four o'clock on the Monday morning; but it was two hours behind its time, and the unfortunate woman was missing. Her body was found in the canal at a place called Brindley's Bank near Rugeley; and there was no doubt about the identity of the body.

Whether she was thrown into the canal, or whether she threw herself in, were not questions for their present consideration; but whether the crime charged upon the prisoners in this indictment had been perpetrated by them. There would be many facts,

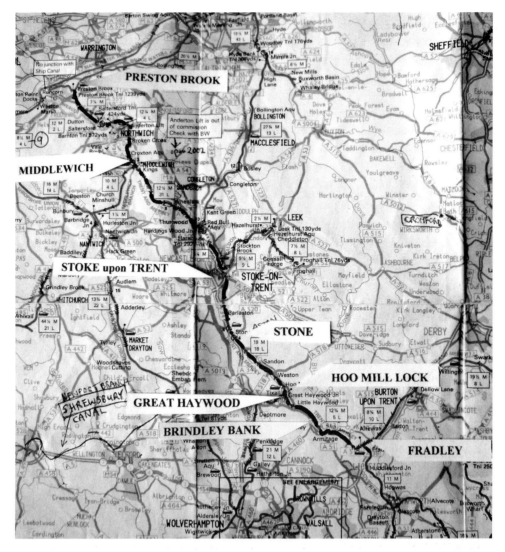

Plan of Christina Collins' journey from Preston Brook to Fradley.

comparatively trifling taken separately, which together they formed a strong body of evidence against them. It would be shown that she was a woman of very decent and tidy appearance, remarkable for attention to her clothes. When her body was found, her clothes were considerably rent and torn, and her drawers particularly were torn in such a way as to show that she had been used with great violence. He had already stated that he should endeavour to obtain the truth from one of the prisoners (Owen) by admitting him as a witness. Those who conducted this prosecution had no other object in adopting that course than to satisfy public justice; and perhaps he might say that this prosecution should stand or fall in some degree by the statement that Owen might give.

Soon after Mr Sergeant Ludlow had concluded his opening, Owen on being asked, said he would not give evidence.

Mr Sergeant Ludlow observed that he was not surprised to hear him say so, as he had observed the attorney for the prisoners more than once in communication with him. The witnesses were then called.

Robert Collins, husband to Christina Collins, the deceased, entered the witness box in a state of great excitement and distress. He wept aloud and seemed as if he could scarcely bare the sight of the prisoners at the bar. He said that he was living in London on the 15th of June, having left his wife in Liverpool at the latter end of April, when he went to London to seek for work. He wrote for his wife to come to London, and sent her a sovereign, all the money he had, in order to enable her to accomplish the journey. In consequence of some information he came into Staffordshire and saw his wife's dead body at Rugeley at the time of the inquest. He could speak positively of the body. For although it was dreadfully disfigured – here the poor fellow could not at all restrain his feelings – yet he knew it by a mark on the ear. His wife's name was Christina Collins.

Elizabeth Grice stated that the wife of the last witness, Christina Collins came to lodge with her at her house in Liverpool, in May last. She was a dressmaker. She recollected her leaving for London on the 15th of June. She had not very good clothes; but they were always neat and in a good state of repair. She had a dark coloured gown; a fawn coloured handkerchief over her neck; and a figured blue silk bonnet with a light ribbon. She left about ten o'clock in the morning. She had not observed that anything was the matter with her elbows. She had never heard her complain of anything of the kind. She wore long sleeves. She was a very delicate kind of person.

Cross-examined by Mr Godson – The witness never heard her say anything about being on the stage, or being connected with Covent Garden Theatre.

Elizabeth Grice. No.

William Brookes, a porter in the employ of Messrs Pickford at Stoke Upon Trent, said that he was examined before the Coroner on Sunday the 16th of June; the three prisoners came to Stoke Upon Trent about twelve o'clock in the day, with one of Pickford's boats containing a cargo of goods, part for London and part for Stoke. Owen was the captain of the boat, the two others were hands employed in navigating her. He also saw a female passenger who had come by the same boat. Whilst the boat remained at Stoke to be unloaded, that female made a complaint to witness. Thomas or Dobell, had said something to the woman, and witness heard her say 'Leave me alone. I'll not have anything to do with you.' After the woman made her complaint, Dobell used some disgraceful language – The witness repeated the language, which was very obscene, and showed an intention to accomplish his desires upon her. When the boat started about four o'clock, the same woman passenger left in it. She had a dark coloured dress on.

Cross-examined by Mr Yardley – He should think the woman was in the presence of the prisoners about the bank and wharf about three hours, whilst the boat remained at Stoke. He thought Dobell had had some drink. The prisoners went away from the wharf an hour after dinner time.

Ann Brookes, wife of the last witness, proved that she went about three and a half miles in the boat from Stoke. A female passenger was on board who seemed poorly. Witness was not much in her company, and she did not make any particular complaint to her.

Cross-examined by Mr Godson – There was a place in the middle of the boat for passengers called 'the hole'.

Hugh Cordwell, check clerk to the Trent and Mersey Canal Company at Stone, proved that the boat was at Stone at eight o'clock on Sunday evening, the 16th of June last: the three prisoners were with the boat. He saw a female in the boat: she made a complaint to him, and he thought Dobell was near enough to hear it. She said 'She was afraid the men were getting drunk and would meddle with her.' Witness replied – 'In case they did, when she got to her journey's end she must report them to their masters.' The boat left Stone at eleven minutes past eight o'clock.

Cross-examined by Mr Godson – They were not sober. Owen had walked through the town, and he came up with a man named Groucott. He asked the woman why she did not follow him through the town? She made no reply.

Cross-examined by Mr Yardley – Groucott left Stone in the boat with them.

John Tansley, assistant clerk to the Trent and Mersey Canal Company at Aston Lock, about a mile from Stone, said that he saw the dead body of a female at the Coroner's inquest at Rugeley; he had seen the same woman alive at half past eight on Sunday Evening, the 16th of June last; she sat on the door of the lock house: she was sharpening a knife. The three prisoners had the charge of the boat. One of the hands, he did not know which, 'Cursed her eyes, and wished she was in hell flames, for he hated the sight of her.' He saw her get on the boat. Owen told her to get on the cabin, and she did so.

Cross-examined by Mr Godson – He did not know whether the woman drank anything at Aston. He saw her put a cup to her mouth but could not tell whether she drank.

By the Judge – Owen gave her the cup.

Thomas Bloor said he was a boatman in the employ of Pickford and Co; he passed along the canal with a boat on Sunday evening the 16th of June between Burston and Sandon, he passed Owen's boat between eight and nine o'clock. Owen and Dobell stood in the hatches. There were two women on board; one sat on the cabin, and the other on the boat. As the boat passed, witness said to Owen 'How goes it?' and asked him to have a glass of ale. Instead of Owen, Dobell jumped on the boat for the ale. Owen pointed to the woman on the cabin and said something. Witness gave the words of Owen, and his own reply, which we forbear to repeat.

Dobell said 'he would — her that night or he would — her' – (A sensation of horror throughout the court.) Owen was quite intoxicated and Dobell was rather so. Witness did not see anything of Ellis.

Cross-examined by Mr Godson – Witness was quite sober at the time. They were having some ale on their boat; they had taken a gallon on board at Haywood, it being the wakes, and there were six of them to drink it.

Cross-examined by Mr Yardley – Dobell was not drunk.

Robert Walker, boatman of Shardlow, said that on Sunday night, the 16th of June, he was steering a boat about half a mile below Sandon Lock about ten o'clock at night. He met a boat, and about four or five hundred yards before the boat he had seen a woman walking on the towing path. He could not swear to anyone with the boat to be confident. There was an inquiry made of him by some person on board that boat.

Mr Godson, Mr Yardley and **Mr Beadon** objected to this line of examination. There was no proof that this was the boat on board of which the prisoners were. Considerable discussion took place and – **Mr Justice Williams** thought the counsel for the prosecution ought to carry the point of the identity of the boat farther.

In the examination of several succeeding witnesses therefore this point was particularly referred to; and his Lordship at length said that the hour and the place corresponded so exactly that he should admit the further evidence of Robert Walker. Hugh Cordwell, the check clerk at the lock at Stone, being recalled, proved that the next boat of Pickford's which left Stone after Owen's, left at half past eleven at night, and he saw no female passenger on board.

Robert Walker then said that someone on board the boat in question asked him 'Where he met the female passenger of theirs.' Witness replied 'Not far before' 'Because' (the man said) 'We want to — her.'

Cross-examined – Did not know who made that enquiry.

Hoo Mill Lock, where the lockkeeper and his wife were woken by the commotion in the lock.

Catherine Tansley, whose father keeps the lock at Sandon, proved that the boat to which the three prisoners belonged, passed through their lock that night, about ten minutes to ten. She saw a woman at the side who got into the boat before it left the lock.

James Mills, the keeper of the Hoo Mill Lock, proved that he and his wife were alarmed by a noise about 12 o'clock at night. Hoo Mill Lock is about five miles from Sandon Lock. It was a cry of distress which they heard. Witness got up to the window. He saw three men by the lock side, and a woman on the cabin of a boat, which was in the lock. It was one of Pickford's; he could tell by the name plate. The woman got off the boat and asked for her shoes. One of the men got on board the boat. While the woman was on the cabin, her legs hung by the side. The woman said – 'I'll not go in; don't attempt me.' The man that stood aside the cabin said – 'Mind her legs.' He recollected his wife making enquiry from the window, and asking what woman they had on board. One of the men said 'A passenger.'

Cross-examined by Mr Godson – His wife asked if she had anyone belonging to her on board. The man replied 'Her husband.'

Ann Mills, wife of the last witness, said she was part asleep and part awake on the night in question; when she heard what she first thought was the cry of a child. She got up to the window, and saw a boat of Pickford's in the lock: it was going towards London. There was a woman sitting on the cabin; she was crying. She heard her crying. She saw three men about the boat. She asked the men what was amiss. One of the men said – 'She's been in the cut.' She got off the cabin and cried out for her shoes. She appeared to have a dark gown on. There was a man in the hatches where they stand to steer; she could not see whether the woman had her cap or her shoes on. Then she got on the outside of the cabin with her legs hanging down. She said 'Don't tempt me; I'll not go down; I'll not go near you.' A man on the side said 'Mind her legs.' Witness called a man who was on the lock side to her and asked him what woman they had on board. He answered 'A passenger.' Witness asked him if there was anybody with her, and he said 'Her husband.' Another boat came into the lock the other way as soon as the Pickford's boat left.

Cross-examined by Mr Godson – Pickford's have a great many boats on the canal. When the man said 'Mind her legs' she supposed he meant lest they should be hurt by the boat going down in the lock.

Joseph Littlemore, a boatman in the employ of Messrs Worthington. He was going through the Hoo Mill lock about 12 o'clock on the night in question, and met one of Pickford's boats just coming out. Two men got upon the boat below the lock. An enquiry was made by a female from Mills house window.

Cross-examined by Mr Godson – He should think Pickford's had one hundred boats on this canal. The boats occasionally pass each other. The average speed of travelling is about three miles an hour; sometimes it is less; sometimes it is four miles.

James Willday, captain of one of Bache and Co's boats, was going to London on the night in question. Their boat passed the Hoo Mill lock about 12 o'clock. He knew Owen, but did not see anything of him until about three o'clock in the morning, when they came to the bridge below Handsacre. Owen's was the first of Pickford's boats that he had overtaken that morning. He saw Owen jump off and go into the cabin. The cabin doors were closed immediately as he went in. Musson was steering the boat. Witness went on his way to London.

Cross-examined by Mr Godson – He should think Handsacre was nine miles from the Hoo Mill lock. They had passed by Rugeley.

William Hatton was driving the boat, of which the last witness was captain on the morning in question. He drove from Colwich Lock to Armitage tunnel. They overtook Owen's boat at Rugeley Wharf between one and two o'clock in the morning. That is five or six miles from the Hoo Mill lock. He met Owen on the towing path; Dobell was with him. Dobell had no jacket on nor waistcoat. One of them asked witness 'If he had seen a woman?' He said he had not. They asked him again – 'If he had seen one anywhere' and he said no. They asked him a third time 'If he had seen one between there and the turnover bridge.' He said he had not seen one anywhere. That place was four or five hundred yards from Brindley's Bank. Witness's boat had passed Brindley's Bank. After they had made those enquiries they went on after their own boat.

Cross-examined by Mr Yardley – Their boat was not in sight when they made those enquiries; they were coming away from it, but returned, insisting that he had seen nothing of the woman.

William Musson, the boy who was originally charged with the other prisoners, was next placed in the witness box. He stated that he was on one of Pickford's boats on the 15th of June which Owen was the captain. Dobell and Ellis were two men who assisted in working her. They four were the crew of the boat. They took a passenger from Preston Brook: Witness was there when the woman came on board. He was before the Coroner, and saw the body of a woman. She was the same woman that they took on board at Preston Brook. She had two bundles with her, two boxes and a roll. The boxes were corded with light coloured cord. Witness saw the woman sharpening a penknife at Aston Lock. When witness got out of bed about half past one, he left Owen and the woman in the cabin, about a mile from Colwich Lock. That is nearer Rugeley than Hoo Mill lock. When witness went to bed, nobody was in the cabin but himself. The woman was at the top of the cabin; Dobell was steering; and the other two were at the top of the cabin. Witness woke about half a mile above Colwich lock. He got up and dressed himself and went to work. He was now awake at Hoo Mill lock. Witness missed the woman between three and four o'clock in the morning. He asked Owen where the woman was. He said 'He was affeared she was drowned.' Witness drove the horse from Colwich lock to Brindley's Bank. Ellis was then on the bed asleep; Owen was steering; and Dobell stood on the footboard. At Armitage tunnel, he saw Owen in the 'hole' and he saw the woman's big black box open. He knew Willday. He passed them that morning, and he spoke to witness. Witness shut the cabin door at that time by the captain's orders.

That was near Handsacre, five or six miles from Colwich lock. Ellis and Dobell were in the cabin when the door was shut. They stopped at Rugeley wharf about half an hour. Witness was apprehended at Fazeley. When Ellis got up just above Fradley, Owen told him 'He feared the woman was drowned.' He had not heard Dobell say anything to Ellis since they had been in gaol about this woman. He never heard the woman call out the name of 'Collins'. At Aston lock, Dobell said 'He wished he had never seen her; he hated the sight of her.'

Cross-examined by Mr Godson – Witness drove from Colwich lock to Brindley's Bank. It was about one o'clock when he began to drive; he last saw the woman alive at Colwich lock in the cabin. It was the captain's turn to steer, and the turn of the other two men to go to bed. The place for the passengers is in the middle of the boat. A person at the steerage could not see a passenger in the 'hole'. There were blankets and counterpanes for the use of the woman; he saw her in the 'hole' at Stoke; he frequently saw the woman in the cabin; he saw her lying down in the cabin at Middlewich; she had got her shoes, her bonnet and shawl off. The captain borrowed six shillings to pay Dobell his wages, they having had a few words.

Cross-examined by Mr Yardley – Dobell said he wished 'He had never seen the woman.' Owen wanted to admit the woman into the cabin, and the others objected to it. That was the occasion on which Dobell made use of those words.

Fradley Junction – Trent & Mersey Canal, *c.* 1950.

Cross-examined by Mr Beadon – Ellis was asleep at Brindley's Bank; and when he awoke at Fradley, he could not believe that the woman was drowned: he went into the hole to look for her.

John Bladen was in the employ of the Trent and Mersey Navigation Company; his station was at Rugeley; it was on the 17th June last. It was the duty of a captain who might lose a passenger or goods to report the loss at the next station he came to. There is a way bill with each boat; and if anything is short or wrong, it is usual to make a memorandum on that way bill. When Owen's boat passed the wharf on Monday morning, the 17th of June, no notice was given to him of any loss.

Cross-examined by Mr Godson – He was the person to whom Owen had told something. He had been to the gaol to see Owen. Re-examined by Mr Sergeant Ludlow – he took an account from Musson of what he had to say on the melancholy subject. Owen had said something that morning in his presence; he had said he was willing to give evidence.

Charles Robotham was clerk to Pickford and Co at Fradley Junction. On the 17th June, it was nearly six o'clock in the morning before Owen's boat came up. It ought have been there at four o'clock. Owen came to witness and told him he had had a passenger at Preston Brook, and he believed she was off her head; and she attempted to do it once, and he had pulled her out. Witness told him 'If he thought she had been off her head he ought to have taken better care of her, and kept her in the boat.' Witness asked him where he saw her last? He said 'At Colwich lock.' He said she had left her bonnet and shoes in the cabin. Witness asked him 'What brought her in the cabin?' He then wished witness to take her luggage out of the boat. Witness said if he knew she was drowned, he would. In consequence of what the boy said, witness went on to Fazeley, to see Mr Kirk on the subject. They got the constables and had them taken up. Between seven and eight o'clock that same evening, witness saw Dobell and Ellis, and he asked them where they saw the woman last. He believed they said at Brindley's Bank.

Cross-examined by Mr Godson – Owen said he had been back looking for the woman. At Fazeley he burst out crying and said 'I am innocent.'

Cross-examined by Mr Yardley – Dobell and Ellis said they objected to having the woman in the cabin

William Kirk – agent to Messrs Pickford at Fazeley, said that in consequence of information received from the last witness, he took an opportunity of seeing the prisoners. He saw Ellis first. He went out of the office to tell him to come in. He wanted to speak to him. Witness did not say anything about the woman. Ellis began to curse and swear and said 'Damn and blast the woman, if she is drowned, I cannot help it.' Witness afterward saw Owen. He said 'Owen you have had a female passenger from Preston Brook to London; what has become of her?' He replied – 'It is a very bad job; I'm afraid she is drowned.' He asked him where her luggage was and he said 'In the boat.' And it was given up at Fazeley. Her bonnet, a pair of shoes and clogs were brought out of the cabin. The bonnet appeared as if it had been pulled off a person's head by force. The strings were not untied, and the crown was forced in. Dobell came into the office; he swore and said 'He hoped the bloody w——e was in hell.' Witness gave them into custody.

William Harrison, Constable of Fazeley, recollected being sent for by Mr Kirk on the morning of the 17th. He took Ellis in charge. He began to damn and blast the woman and said 'What do I know about the woman; if she had a mind to drown herself, she might.' He was drunk. He asked the captain what kind of person she was? He said she was 'A little fierce talking woman – a nice little woman.' And that she had a mark on her forehead. Owen was in his custody at Rugeley and he said, 'the woman wanted very little drowning.' He said at the same time that Dobell 'raped the woman and murdered her.'

Cross-examined by Mr Yardley – Owen said that repeatedly. He could not tell what part of the day it was. It was up in a room. He did not recollect that anyone was present except himself. He mentioned it very soon after. He did not know when he mentioned it, but it was to a brother officer.

Cross-examined by Mr Beadon – boatmen swear a great deal, and make use of very coarse language.

(Harrison produced the bonnet and shoes of the deceased.)

Francis Jackson said he had the charge of Owen on the 17th June. He was handcuffed to him on the evening of that day. He saw a person of the name of Robinson. Owen said to Robinson, 'You go and tell the prisoners in the hole to say that we left the woman at Colwich lock.' Witness saw Robinson again in the morning. Owen asked whether he had told them. Robinson said he had. Owen said, 'Go and tell them again.'

Cross-examined by Mr Godson – Witness did not know whether this was said in a whisper, but he heard it.

Henry Sketchley, a labourer of Rugeley, said that on the 22nd of June, Dobell was handcuffed to him in an upper room at the Swan. He remembered standing at the window, when some noise was made by the people in the street. Someone said, 'The captain is coming out against Dobell.' Dobell slept with witness that night. He asked witness whether the captain had come out with anything. Witness replied 'No.' Dobell said 'He had nothing to come out with; that the captain had murdered the woman.' He said 'He – (Dobell) – and Ellis got into the cabin to lie down on this side

Modern Fradley, showing the Swan in winter.

Colwich lock; that Owen was steering and the boy was driving. He was awoke with a cry of 'Oh my Collins! I will jump. Give me my shoes.' Owen said, 'You bloody old cow, if you don't jump, I'll send you off.' Dobell continued in witness's custody till the Monday morning. On the Monday following, Dobell said 'The captain was a bloody rogue, for letting the boy take liberties with the woman.'

John Wood, Constable of Rugeley, said he was present at the inquest, and that two boxes were delivered to him. He searched the contents of one of the boxes and found a penknife in it. The box appeared to have been broken open.

(The penknife was produced.)

Thomas Brandt – a boatman, said that he was on the canal near Brindley's Bank a little after 5 o'clock in the morning on the 17th June. Sixty or seventy yards nearer to Rugeley than Brindley's Bank, he saw something in the water; he saw a gown. It was not on the towing path side, but on the other. He stopped his boat, and with his boat hook towed it over to the towing path. It was the body of a female. It had no bonnet or shoes on. She had a cap on her forehead and a dark gown on. Before he disturbed the body, the head was lying in the direction of Preston Brook. She was lying on her face, which was quite black. He did not think it possible for a woman to jump from a boat in the middle of the canal to the place where the body was found.

Cross-examined by Mr Godson – The canal there might be wide enough for four boats to pass. A boat is about six feet wide. If a boat was passing along the middle of the canal he thought a young man might jump to the place where the body was found, but not a female.

John Johnson, of Bellamour Wharf, said that he remembered the last witness calling his attention to the body of the woman in the canal on the 17th June. The water was about 9 inches deep where the body was found, and it went gradually deeper into the middle from that place. Witness took the body out of the canal.

Hannah Phillips of Rugeley, said that she was employed with the other two women to take the clothes off the body of the woman which was found in the canal; her left sleeve was ripped out of the gathers, and also at the back; the cuff on one hand was also ripped; a small chintz muslin handkerchief was also ripped on each shoulder. By the word ripped, she meant torn.

Cross-examined by Mr Godson – These rips were not as if a boat hook had done them.

Brandt and **Johnson** were recalled, and they stated that they did not tear any of the clothes of the deceased with the boat hook, or in any other way when they got her out of the water.

Elizabeth Matthews said she was engaged to assist in taking off the clothes of the deceased; she particularly noticed the state of her drawers; they were much torn.

(The drawers were produced in court and in front they were torn from side to side.)

Mr Lee said he would first examine Mr Fowke, the Coroner.

Robert Fowke, Esq., was then examined. He stated that he was an attorney, living at Stafford, and one of the coroners of the county. He held an inquest on the body of Christina Collins, at Rugeley. He remembered the three prisoners making certain statements; those statements were reduced to writing and read over to the prisoners, who signed them; Owen with his name and the others with their crosses; they had previously been sworn.

Cross-examined by Mr Godson – The three were in custody at the time. They were not handcuffed; they had been handcuffed, but they were not handcuffed whilst being examined.

Re-examined by Mr Lee – the prisoners expressed their desire to be examined.

Mr Godson contended that the practice was to receive any voluntary statements which accused persons might choose to give. It might indeed happen that parties might be examined upon oath, who might afterwards turn out to be the perpetrators of the crime; in which case there was some excuse for having them examined upon oath; but in the present instance, the men were in close custody, and yet were examined upon oath. He contended that their depositions taken under such circumstances were not legal evidence and could not be read.

Mr Justice Williams said his own opinion was that they could be read, and he would allow them to be read; but he would certainly reserve the point for the opinion of the judges. It will be remembered that at the inquest, the prisoners were examined several different times.

Mr Bellamy, jun, proceeded to read their depositions as follows:

George Thomas, alias Dobell, of Wombourne, boatman, sworn – I have seen the body; it is that of the woman who was passenger in our boat. James Owen, Wm Lambert, the boy and myself were the persons who worked the boat. Lambert and myself worked together, and the master and the boy worked together. I steered and Lambert drove the horse to the second bridge, this side Barton Tunnel. The captain, the passenger and the boy were in the cabin. I legged through Barton Tunnel for the master, for which he paid me sixpence. The boy legged with me. Lambert drove and the captain steered. I steered to Change Bridge. The captain then took my place and I went to bed. It was about ten o'clock. The woman was in the cabin; she went out while we undressed, but returned in a short time and lay down on the side bench. I was in bed for about four hours. When I awoke, the deceased was sitting in the cabin. I drove to Wollert pound; I then got on the boat and steered to the Mill pound, and then drove to Tunstall Bridge. I then went into the boat; the woman was sitting in the cabin; she remained there until we came near Stoke, when she got out and walked about three quarters of a mile. She got on the boat again at the bottom lock at Stoke. I filled the locks at Stoke. The woman went into the warehouse while we unloaded the boat, and she went with us to a public house kept by John Machie. We took two or three quarts of porter. The woman did not drink anything. I got into the boat at Stoke and went to sleep; I don't know whether the woman got in or not. When the boat arrived at Stone, she was sitting on it. She got off at Stone and walked to Aston lock. She was on the lock side when we got there. The lad was driving and he filled the lock. The deceased wanted to get into the cabin at Aston, but Lambert and I would not let her, and she sat on the top. Gailey left us at Aston lock. The deceased rode on the boat down the Weston pound, and I sat on the boat. I should have been driving, but the horse went of himself. The captain and the boy were then in the cabin in bed; Lambert was steering. When we got to the Hoo Mill lock, the woman wanted to get into the cabin, but I would not let her, and she screamed out. The captain looked out and ordered her into the cabin; she went into the cabin. About 20 minutes afterwards I looked into the cabin and saw her in bed with the captain; both the captain and the woman were dressed; the boy was undressed. The woman remained in the cabin with the captain from the Hoo Mill lock till we arrived at Colwich lock. The captain then got up to steer and the boy to drive. Lambert and I went into the cabin and went to bed. The woman was then sitting in the cabin. We lay down with our clothes on and went to sleep.

The master called me somewhere betwixt Rugeley and the Armitage tunnel, and told me the woman was missing, and I went with him to look for her. We went to betwixt the watering place and the stopping place at Sandhole turn, when I told Owen I would go no further, and we both turned back. When we were at Hoo Mill

Weston, and the towing path along which Christina walked.

lock, I think the lock-keeper's wife called to us. I was fresh. I never told anyone the deceased had attempted to drown herself. She often shouted out 'Collins – Collins' when she came on board, she said, 'If anyone mislested her, she would make herself away.' I think the deceased could not have got into the water without the steerer seeing her. If she had gone into the boat and had straw like another passenger, ten to one this would not have happened. We passed several boats, but I don't know whose they were.

William Ellis (otherwise called William Lambert) of Brinklow near Coventry, upon his oath saith – I am a boatman; James Owen engaged me about five weeks ago in London. I went with him from London to Preston, and was returning from Preston to London again. The deceased took her passage at Preston Brook for London. I never saw the deceased before I saw her at Preston on Saturday evening at seven o'clock. Owen, Dobell, the boy and myself were the only persons with the boat; we work by turns: I worked with Dobell, and the boy worked with Owen. She got into the cabin at Preston and remained there till we got to Stoke. She got out at Stoke, where the boat stopped about two hours. The woman went into the office and remained there all the time we were at Stoke. I went to Machie's house at Stoke, and had about two quarts of ale. The woman went along with us. The woman did not drink anything; she said she went for company. She did not remain in the place where we were, but went into the back place. She left the house with us. It was porter we drank and not ale. We had not more than two quarts. It was Sunday, between 12 and 1 o'clock in the day. She got on the stern plank end near the cabin. Dobell and myself went into the cabin; we both of us lay down and went to sleep. Owen was steering and the boy was driving. I was called by Owen when we came to Meaford lock. I got up and left Dobell asleep whilst I went to fill the lock. The woman was then on the boat. I walked on to Stone before the boat to get the locks ready. The woman passed me at the Stone lock against the office. We remained at Stone whilst the boat was gauged.

I am certain the woman was not in the boat whilst it was gauged. I did not see the woman again till we came to Aston lock. I saw the woman standing on the lock side when we got there. I was steering the boat. The boy went to fill the lock and the horse was going by itself. Dobell was on the cabin and so was the captain. Dobell and the captain both got off at the lock. Thomas Groucott came with us from Stone. He went about two bridges beyond the lock, and then turned back with another boat. I gave the permit to the clerk at Stone. Groucott got it back before we left. The clerk gauged the boat. The captain did not get off at Aston lock.

When we left Aston lock, I drove and Dobell steered. The woman, the captain and the boy went into the cabin. We went in this way to Sandon lock. We did not stop at Sandon lock longer than to work through it. At Sandon lock, Dobell and myself said the woman ought not to be in the cabin. The captain was then in the middle of the boat and the woman on the cabin. The captain said the woman should go into the cabin and we said it was not a place for her, and she should not go in. When we went to bed at Change Bridge, the woman was in the cabin; she went out while we undressed. Dobell and Owen were disputing about the woman being admitted into the cabin, and Dobell said he would leave, and Owen said he had not got money to pay him. The woman got off the boat at Sandon lock and walked on; she got on the boat again a mile below. She sat on the cabin until we came to Hoo Mill lock, when she went into the cabin, and remained there till we came to Colwich lock, when Dobell called the captain. The woman went out on the hatches; the captain went to steer and the boy to drive, and Dobell and I went to bed. The woman was in the hatches when we went to bed. She was there when the boat left Colwich lock. The captain was steering, and the boy driving the boat through the lock. I should think it was an hour or an hour and a half after we were in bed that the captain called Dobell and said the woman was gone. Dobell got up and went out of the cabin. When we got to Wood End lock, Owen told me that the woman was gone, and they had been back to look for her, but could see nothing of her. I went forward to fill the locks at Hoo Mill lock. I did not hear any noise; I drew the paddles; if there had been any I must have heard it. I steered out of Hoo Mill lock, and Dobell drove. Owen, the woman and the boy were in the cabin. The woman was lying down by Owen. I don't think the woman got off the boat at Hoo Mill lock, I never saw her get off. She might have done so, but I was filling the lock and drawing the paddles. The deceased said several times during the voyage that she would destroy herself. I never heard of her having been in the water. I never saw her with her clothes wet. If her clothes had been put to dry, I think I must have seen them. When she said she would not go to London, she said, 'Oh my Collins'.

I never saw anyone ill treat her. Had I been steering, I think no person could have got out of the boat without my seeing them. I never saw her any more. She seemed very comfortable. She never took anything while she was on board that I know of, except that she had half a pint of rum with her when she came on board at Preston, and she gave some to us. I did not see her drink anything herself. I got in at Colwich lock, and before I went to sleep, I heard Owen call her 'A whore and a cow'.

James Owen of Brinklow near Coventry, upon his oath saith – I have seen the body of the deceased; it is that of the woman who was my passenger from Preston to London. I first missed her at Rugeley; she went into the cabin at Preston. She remained there till we got to Middlewich. Wm Lambert drove from Preston to Barton Tunnel and Thomas steered. I was in the cabin from the time we left Preston till we came to Barton Tunnel, and the boy was with me, and the woman was in her apartment in the middle of the boat. I gave Thomas sixpence to 'leg' for me through Barton Tunnel, and I told the woman she might come into the cabin. I was then steering and Thomas and the boy were legging for me, and Lambert was driving. While they were legging me through the tunnel, I told the woman she might come into the cabin. She said it was very hard for her to have paid sixteen shillings and to have no straw. She said she was very short of money, and that if I would find her victuals, she would satisfy me when we got to London. It was about nine o'clock. When we had passed the tunnel, Lambert and Thomas went to bed. The woman was in the cabin when they went in, and they made no objection to her being there. The woman came out of the cabin into the hatches whilst the men undressed. She went into the cabin when the men were in bed and sat down on the side bed. I could see into it from where I stood. She remained there for some time and then she came out of the cabin and talked to me about plays. She said she belonged to Covent Garden Theatre, and that she would give me a ticket to go there when she got to London. She said she was married to a second husband who was in London. She said she lived in Edgware Road. At Middlewich, Lambert and Thomas got up and myself and the boy went to bed. The woman was in the cabin sitting on the side bed. The boy and myself both undressed in the cabin where the woman was, and when I was in bed I told the woman she might come and lie down by me, which she did. The woman lay down with her clothes on. When we got to Harecastle Tunnel, it was my turn to leg, and I gave a man who was about a shilling to leg for me. It was about nine o'clock in the morning.

I got up and had my breakfast with the woman. Lambert was lying in the cabin asleep, on the side bed. He got in when we came to the tunnel. I steered to Stoke and the lad drove. The woman was sitting on the cabin. She went there from the tunnel to Stoke lock, where she got off. She followed me down the locks to a public house kept by Thomas Lees. We had half a pint of ale apiece there. When we left the public house she went and got on the middle of the boat, where she remained till we came to Stoke wharf. She got out there and went and sat on the steps at the office door. Myself and the men were unloading the boat. At dinner time, between one and two o'clock, the clerks and the porters left the wharf, and we ate some bread and cheese and then went to a public house kept by John Machie. We had three pots and a pint. The woman would not have any porter and sat by the back door while we were in the public house. We were in the public house about an hour. We went to the wharf, loaded the boat, got the invoices and started. The woman rode on the top of the cabin. The ostler's wife and her had rode on the boat from Stoke to the Plume of Feathers at Darlaston, where the ostler's wife left. The deceased seemed low and out of spirits when we left Stoke; and soon after we had left, I told her to go to the hole to the woman and have some chat. She went in to the hole. She remained in the hole till we got to Stone. At Stone I left the boat for about quarter of an hour; I went to buy some bread. The woman was in the hole when I returned to the boat. I don't know whether the woman was in the boat or not when I returned from buying the bread. I was muddled when I came to Stone. I bought the bread at Samuel Gilberts. I don't know whether the woman was on the boat when it left Stone or not. I steered to Stone; the boy was in the hatches with me. Nobody could get out of the hatches without the person who steered knowing it by day light; but they might by night. When I came back with the bread, I put the bread on the cabin. I don't know whether the woman was in the boat or not when the bread was put in the boat. I don't recollect seeing the woman after I had bought the bread until I came to Aston lock. She was then in the cabin. I don't know whether I walked or rode from Stone to Aston. I went to bed at the pound below Aston lock.

When I went to bed, the woman was sitting on the cabin. I gave her two blankets and a counterpane and some clothes to put under her head. I then went into the cabin and went to bed; I put the blankets and the counterpane in the hole and then went to bed. I told her I had put the things there as I went. I had been in bed about two hours and a half when I heard the woman crying in the cabin. Thomas was with

A modern view of Stone Lock.

her in the cabin and Lambert was steering. I jumped out of bed and laid hold of her. She said, 'Oh captain! Oh my Collins! I'll drown myself before I get to London.' I asked her what for. I asked if they had done anything to her; but she kept crying and sobbing very much and made no answer. Thomas was standing by her when I was awoke. Her dress did not appear disordered. I accused the men of having abused her; and they said they had not, and were very saucy, and I threatened to dismiss Thomas. I borrowed 6 shillings from the boy to pay Thomas his wages. I owed him 10 shillings, and I had 4 myself. The boy was asleep along with me in the cabin. It was below Haywood lock.

Whilst I was jawing the men and quieting the woman, the boy got up. The disturbance was between Haywood lock and Colwich lock, and Lambert steered till we came to Colwich church yard, when I went to steer, and Lambert went into the cabin to Thomas. It was at the stop at Brindley's Bank I borrowed the money from the boy. While I was quarrelling with the men, the woman attempted to jump from the hatches into the canal. I caught hold of her and pulled her into the boat. She said she would drown herself before she got to London. She was wet up to her knees. I told her to go into the cabin. Thomas was in the cabin and the other man was steering. Both Thomas and Lambert appeared to be in liquor. She went to the top of the cabin and I remained in the hatches talking to her till we got to Colwich lock. I went in and put on my shoes and stockings and then went and steered to Rugeley, and Lambert went into the cabin to Thomas; the boy was driving.

We had two hampers of wine for Atherstone. When we got to Colwich lock and before I went to put on my shoes and stockings, the woman got off the boat on the contrary side to the towing path and I though she was going to ease herself so I made no remark. I was having words with the men and did not see anything of the woman again. I was jawing and differing with them and did not know she was missing. I met Bache's boat near Brindley's Bank; a man named 'Moneher' was driving. I asked him if had ever seen a woman as I was looking for one. He said no he had not. Thomas was with me. He came with me from Rugeley to look for the woman. I woke Lambert at Rugeley wharf and told him the woman was missing, but he would not come out.

George Thomas, alias Dobell. At Colwich lock, I called the master as it was his turn to work. The boy left the cabin first and went to the horse. The captain and the woman then came out of the cabin; he was using abusive language to the woman, saying we had had connection with her. Afterwards Lambert and myself had some talk about it and then went to sleep. We were disturbed shortly afterwards by hearing words between the captain and the woman, and I heard the woman say – 'I'll jump, I'll jump.' And I heard the captain say – 'You b—r, if you don't I'll throw you off.' When we came to the stop place beyond the turn, I asked the captain if he was not ashamed to turn the woman out. It was half way betwixt the turn and stop place; he told me I might get out if I liked, and called the lad back to borrow some money to pay me. We were wrangling about it until we got close to Rugeley when he began to say the deceased was lost, she was drowned; the boy was present. The captain and I went back to look for the woman. Lambert was in the cabin and did not go. It was about three o'clock in the morning when we were at Rugeley. At Fradley he told Robotham there was a passenger missing, and on the way to Fazeley he wanted me and Lambert to swear that the deceased got out at Colwich lock.

William Ellis, alias Lambert – sworn – As we were coming along the Fazeley pound, Owen asked us to say that the woman got out at Colwich lock. Dobell drove from Aston lock to Sandon lock; he steered and Owen was in the middle of the boat. The boy was on the cross bed, the woman was walking.

Sandon Lock.

James Owen – sworn – At about 12 o'clock on Sunday night, when the boat was below Haywood pound, I was awoke by the noise of the woman. I saw the woman in bed and Thomas upon her. I jawed him about her, and he said that Lambert had had connection with her at the Hoo Mill lock. I was fast asleep in bed at Hoo Mill lock, and did not hear any noise. When we came below Colwich lock, Lambert wanted to take the woman into the cabin, and I would not let him. Dobell and I kept quarrelling about a mile. At Bellamour Crane I told the woman to get on the cabin and go to her apartment; she did so. The last time I saw her alive was at Turnover Bridge, in the middle of the boat. I called the boy into the cabin, and I did not get out until I came to the watering place near Rugeley, when I missed the woman for the first time. When I came to Fazeley pound I went to the hole and saw Lambert and Dobell with one of the passenger's boxes open. I told them I would not go any farther than Fazeley; and they said, 'Go to hell with you. You are frightened about the woman. Tell them she got out at Colwich lock.'

James Owen – sworn – After I had prevented Lambert from taking the deceased to bed, I took her in my arms and put her on the top of the cabin. Lambert was in bed and Thomas sitting on the side bench. The boy was driving and I was steering. About seven or eight or nine minutes after I had put the woman on the cabin, Thomas said, 'Come in damn your eyes and pay me.' I went into the cabin to my cupboard to look for money to pay him, and Thomas went to the helm. I found I was six shillings short, and put my head out of the cabin to call the boy. Thomas was then at the helm, but the woman was missing. I heard a noise while in the cabin, as if someone had jumped on the cabin. It was impossible for anyone to jump on the cabin unless they were in the boat.

Mr Fowke was again asked whether the three prisoners were all present when those respective statements were made? He replied that they were not. They were brought in separately and separately examined.

In reply to a question from **Mr Godson, Mr Fowke** stated that Mr Barnett, surgeon, was examined on the inquest. He was the only surgeon examined.

In reply to **Mr Sergeant Ludlow, Mr Fowke** said he was not aware of anything being said of importance which he did not take down.

James Ruscoe, agent to the Trent and Mersey Canal Co at Stoke, was at Rugeley at the time of the inquest, on the 20th of June. In consequence of a message from Owen, he went to him in a room at a public house. Owen requested witness to take down what he had to say, and he accordingly took it down, and afterwards read it over to him, when he signed his name to it. Witness had now the paper in his hand.

Mr Godson objected to that paper being read. It was a most irregular proceeding to make the attempt. If anyone could take depositions from persons, it would be idle in future to attempt to give solemn proofs of parties having been examined by magistrates, and signing their statements in the presence of the magistrates.

Mr Sergeant Ludlow said: It was one of the first principles recognised in the criminal jurisprudence of the country, that what a person said, might be given in evidence against himself; and if this statement of the prisoner had been made in a letter to Mr Ruscoe, could anyone doubt that the letter would have been evidence.

Mr Justice Williams should not direct the paper to be read by the officer of the court, but if Mr Roscoe chose to aid his memory by referring to the paper, he might do so.

Mr Roscoe then stated that Owen told him that at Haywood lock, he heard the cries of the woman passenger, and Dobell was pulling her about. He said that Dobell and he had some words about her. Ellis and the woman were on the towing path at Hoo Mill lock, and he could not help laughing at some conversation he heard there between Ellis and Dobell, about cutting her trousers. He said that the woman did get out at Colwich lock, but she got on again, and that Ellis at Colwich lock got hold of her, and wanted to take her to bed, and he (Owen) would not let him. That the woman told him that they had been pulling her about; that in consequence of that he was falling out with them about the woman. He said that Ellis was asleep when the boat got to Rugeley; that the woman got on the boat at Bellamour Crane; that she then got into the middle of the boat; that he then called the boy Musson on board, and borrowed 6 shillings off him to pay Dobell his wages; that he then saw the woman's shoes and bonnet: that he then went to the middle of the boat to look for her. That was by the stop place at Brindley's Bank: that the woman at that time was not there; in consequence of which he gave the alarm to his men; that Dobell, Ellis and he (the captain) returned to look for the woman till they came to a boat driven by a man named Moucher. They then turned back; that Ellis would not believe it when he told him that she was missing; that Ellis went to the middle of the boat to look for her; that Ellis went a second time to look for her. That Ellis said to him (Owen) he seemed very much frightened; but they must all say that she got out at Colwich lock, and they could say no more.

Mr Sergeant Ludlow. That is my case my lord.

Mr Godson. Then I contend that it is no case at all.

Mr Justice Williams said he had forborne to say a single word until his brother Ludlow had declared that that was his case. He would indeed have sat till midnight, nay till tomorrow night, and the next night to patiently hear any evidence that might be adduced in support of this charge. But how could he allow a case like this to go to the jury, when there was not one particle of evidence to showing that any rape had been committed on the woman at all. That it was a case abounding with circumstances of suspicion was perfectly true; but there was no more evidence of rape, than of murder, and it became his duty to say, that he thought there was not a case to go to the jury.

Mr Sergeant Ludlow said – The case was certainly altered when he was interrupted in carrying out his intention of examining Owen. He believed it was his duty to bow to the decision of his Lordship.

Mr Justice Williams to the jury – Gentleman, I in common with you, may suppose that foul play took place on board that boat and about it that night. We may imagine that dreadful deeds were done that night with regard to this unhappy woman; but in this realm of England we do not go on mere suspicion, we do not convict except the charge is supported by proofs applicable thereto. The charges in this case are –that all three ravished this unhappy woman; the charges being laid in various forms; but where is the evidence that this unhappy woman was ravished at all. You have not heard one word about the state of her person. There is no proof of any violence having been committed upon her. It is true that Owen is said to have stated that Dobell had 'raped and murdered her' but whatever suspicion that language may raise in your minds and mine, it is no evidence in law against Dobell; nor is the statement of any one of the prisoner's evidence against another, though it is evidence against himself. Supposing you had been trying them for the crime of murder, the evidence is as appropriate to convict them all as of rape. Whatever we may suspect, and whatever may be at the bottom of the hearts of those men, to accompany them to their latest day in life, aye and beyond it, I am bound to tell you that there is no proof of them having committed the crime of which they stand charged in this indictment.

Mr Sergeant Ludlow then submitted that there was abundant evidence of assault, the state of the clothes, and the declarations of the parties, beside the fact disclosed in the investigation that they 'were pulling her about' would be sufficient evidence to prove an assault.

Mr Godson replied that the only evidence, even of an assault would be from the declarations of the men against each other, which in fact were not evidence.

The judge decided against Mr Sergeant Ludlow; and the jury under his Lordship's direction, found a verdict of '**Not Guilty**'.

THE TRIAL FOR MURDER POSTPONED UNTIL THE NEXT ASSIZES

Mr Sergeant Ludlow had an application to make to the court.

He applied that the trial of these men on the indictment for the murder of the unfortunate woman Christina Collins might be postponed until the next Assizes, on the ground that if the trial was now proceeded with, a most material piece of evidence would be wanting. An affidavit on the subject was in preparation, which would be ready for his lordship's consideration in a very short time.

Mr Godson, and the other council for the prisoners resisted the application.

Mr Justice Williams said however that he would receive the affidavit.

Mr Lee spoke to his lordship privately, and informed him, we presume, of the nature of the evidence referred to.

Mr Sergeant Ludlow shortly afterwards presented the affidavit, it was that of John Horton, the attorney for the prosecution: and it set forth that Joseph Orgill was a material and necessary witness in the case, and that it would not be safe to proceed to the trial of the said murder without Joseph Orgill as a witness. That Joseph Orgill was undergoing punishment in the county Gaol, and could not now be admitted as a witness; but before the next Assizes, application would be made to the Secretary of State for a free pardon for the said Joseph Orgill, and if that was obtained, he would be a competent witness.

Mr Sergeant Ludlow said, on that affidavit he applied for the postponement of the trial.

Mr Godson said he hoped his lordship would do no such thing as put off the trial of these men on such grounds. This Joseph Orgill had been convicted of bigamy at the present Assizes, and he was now undergoing the just punishment of the law. How could it be supposed that he was a necessary witness to the case? He knew nothing of the unfortunate woman, the cause of whose death they would have to enquire into. It was not pretended that there was anything whatever to connect Orgill with this melancholy transaction. If this course was adopted, convicted felons would think they had nothing to do but to trump up some tale against a prisoner, still untried, in order to have a remission of punishment. It would in fact be a bonus on falsehood and perjury: and he hoped his lordship would set no example of such a tendency, by allowing this man to become a witness under such circumstances. This was strange indeed. Why his learned friends had asked his lordship to have these men found guilty of a common assault, in which case, of course the indictment for murder would have been set aside. Upon the suggestion of a felon, however, of something that had occurred in gaol, this extraordinary application was made. He trusted his lordship would not comply with the application.

Mr Yardley would only add one word more to what had been properly urged by his learned friend. Here was an application for the postponement of a trial in order that a witness might be brought forward who had shown himself in a peculiar manner disqualified to give evidence. He had pledged himself under the holiest sanction to a poor woman, whilst at the same time, he was practicing upon her the grossest fraud.

Mr Beadon followed in support of the objection.

Mr Sergeant Ludlow replied that it was not a question now, but it would be hereafter, to what degree of credit this man was entitled; and then he supposed the arguments of his learned friends would be reiterated with many variations. The affidavit he had presented expressed the belief of the person making it, that the ends of justice would be furthered if the present application was complied with. He thought after the facts which had been disclosed with reference to that dismal case which his lordship had been occupied so many hours in hearing, his lordship would think that the ends of justice would be furthered by the postponement of this trial. Why they were all aware of a case of rape in which the trial had absolutely been put off until a child grew older and became instructed, so as to be a competent witness; and twelve months ago, on this circuit, a trial at Oxford for murder had been put off on the ground of the indisposition of a witness. In fact the application was quite in the ordinary course of things.

Mr Justice Williams said – In considering this application; it was impossible to separate in his mind the melancholy facts which had been elicited in the late investigation, and although he had felt it his duty to tell the jury in that case that it was impossible for them to find a verdict under that indictment, yet it could not be concealed that there was already a most serious case of suspicion against these men. That being under his cognizance, he felt disposed to grant the application on the affidavit that material evidence might be obtained from a person therein named. On this application therefore, with a view to the justice of the country, he should postpone the trial for murder until the next assizes.

Mr Godson then applied for the discharge of the indictments for assault and felonious stealing, but his lordship said they must stand over.

It is only proper to state that this case throughout was conducted with great ability. The learned council both for the prosecution and the defence, displayed their customary legal knowledge and acumen, and exerted themselves to the utmost in the discharge of their duty.

Mr Horton of Rugeley, solicitor for the prosecution, was awarded by Mr Justice Williams the sum of £10 and 5 Shillings, for the vigorous manner in which he had taken up the case; and the counsel we believe expressed their strong approval of the briefs, and the manner in which the prosecution was got up. Indeed the report of the trial proves that extraordinary pains had been taken to make the chain of evidence as complete as possible.

IN THE NISI PRIUS COURT TUESDAY

Before Mr Baron Alderson

The first prisoner called up was Joseph Orgill to receive judgment, having been convicted of bigamy the previous day. In addressing him, his lordship observed that he had had considerable difficulty in deciding whether he should not transport him. His was not an ordinary case. It was surrounded with circumstances of very great aggravation. He was a married man, a married man too with four children, and while in a foreign country, in utter disregard of all the sacred obligations by which he was both bound as a husband and a father, he had wickedly insinuated himself into the good opinion of a deserving and unsuspecting female, and had induced her to become his wife.

At this instance, Eliza Nagle rushed into the witness box, and was about to address his lordship in extenuation, when she was prevented, and his lordship proceeded.

THE MURDER OF CHRISTINA COLLINS NEWS REPORT

Joseph Orgill, a prisoner who had been convicted of bigamy, and sentenced to 18 months imprisonment, was then by the direction of the judge placed at bar, and Mr Bellamy, the clerk of the Arraigns addressing him said that Her Majesty had been pleased to grant him her most gracious pardon, in order to enable him to give evidence in the case of James Owen, and others, charged with the wilful murder of Christina Collins. 'And it is hoped,' added Mr Bellamy, 'You will make a proper return for this mercy by stating the truth, the whole truth, and nothing but the truth.'

Orgill acknowledged this admonition by a bow, and was then sworn to give evidence before the grand jury.

CHAPTER 7

Life in Stafford Gaol for Owen, Thomas and Ellis

The first reference to a county gaol appears in the Crown records of 1185, which was the probable year of construction. Made of timber or maybe wattle, it was repaired at least two times between 1194 and 1221, but references then cease for fifty years, probably because, in the thirteenth century, Staffordshire and Shropshire formed a single bailiwick, and Stafford prisoners were kept at Bridgnorth or Shrewsbury due to the possibility that Stafford Gaol may collapse. Repaired in 1272, it resumed delivery of felons in 1285, and was repaired twice more before being abandoned, while the 'lock up' was established at the town gates. Old records state,

> Stafford at the north gate, three rooms for men and two for women. A room below called the dungeon with four apertures about four inches square. No employment; prisoner always shut up and in irons; the small court not secure.

A few years later, it was reported that 'men and women were separated at night, although they shared one small dayroom. In the dungeon for male felons, fifty-two were chained down with fourteen inches of space each; however, there was a good lofty store room.'

Fifty-two may not seem a significant number, but at this time, the total number of prisoners in the country was small. In 1779, Howard estimated this at 4,375, of which at least half were debtors.

The first Stafford Gaol on the present site was erected in 1793, following the act of 1791, which was the first to recommend cellular confinement. The beginnings of what is now the Crescent Building were begun in the 1830s, as the house of correction with 175 cells. It was not until 1864 that this was increased to 304 cells. What is now the Main Hall was built in 1845, and the women's wing – now the young prisoner's wing – in 1851. The prison passed into the hands of the government in 1877 and was closed in 1916. Many attempts to re-purchase it were resisted and it was reopened in 1939 after the bombing of Liverpool Gaol.

On entering the gaol in the mid-nineteenth century, an official at the Lodge would take the prisoners down to the reception room where they would be handed over to the clerk. He takes notes of their names, age, sex, and any previous convictions, and then hands them over to another officer, who conducts them to the bath. This is the first compulsory process of discipline and is worse to many prisoners than all the other hardships to come. A similar process to the workhouse now ensues when their clothes are removed, ticketed, placed on a rack, and they are issued with a prison suit.

RULES, ORDERS,

AND

REGULATIONS

FOR THE

GOVERNMENT of the GAOL,

FOR THE

COUNTY of STAFFORD.

Made and confirmed at a General Quarter Seffions of the Peace, holden at STAFFORD, in and for the faid County, on THURSDAY, the 17th Day of January, 1793.

Stafford Gaol Rule Book.

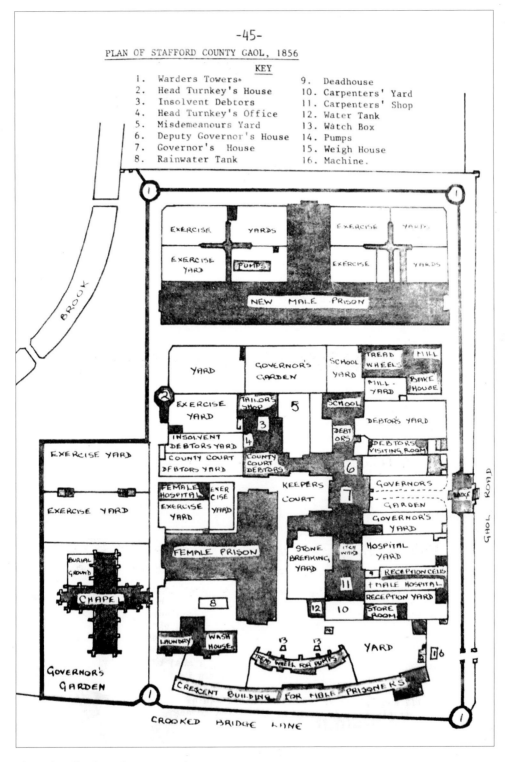

-45-

PLAN OF STAFFORD COUNTY GAOL, 1856

KEY

1. Warders Towers*
2. Head Turnkey's House
3. Insolvent Debtors
4. Head Turnkey's Office
5. Misdemeanours Yard
6. Deputy Governor's House
7. Governor's House
8. Rainwater Tank
9. Deadhouse
10. Carpenters' Yard
11. Carpenters' Shop
12. Water Tank
13. Watch Box
14. Pumps
15. Weigh House
16. Machine.

Plan of Stafford Gaol – nineteenth century.

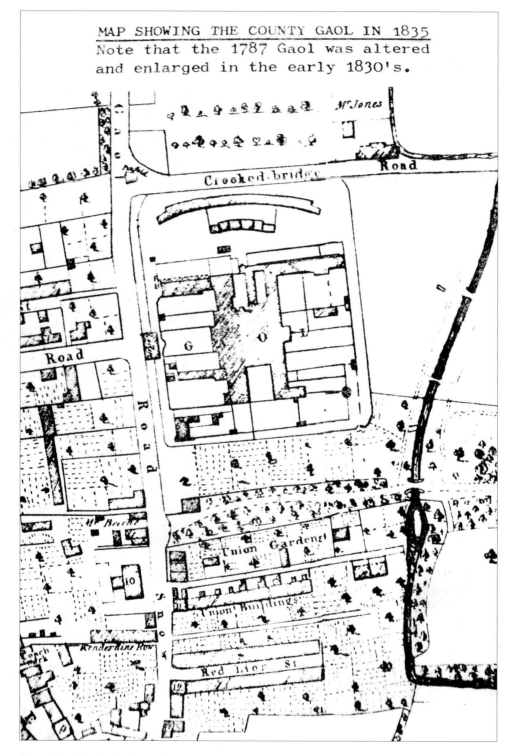

Plan of Stafford and the gaol.

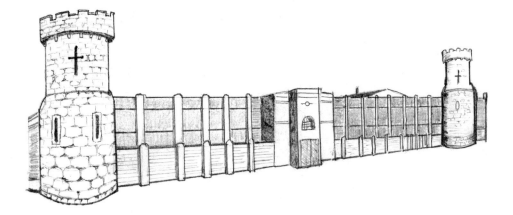

Stafford Prison at the time of the three boatmen.

Stafford Gaol today.

Trent & Mersey Canal near Handsacre.

After being examined by the surgeon as to fitness, they are then taken to their individual cells and checked again to make sure that nothing has been concealed.

Each day they are put to work – which lasts for some ten hours, eight probably on the 'crank' or treadmill or 'picking oakum', which canal students may know is a fibrous material used in the past for caulking seams on wooden boats before covering with tar. Each day, they are marched from their cells in gangs to the mill.

This instrument of torture was built like a large drum with steps fixed upon it every 8-10 inches. Each man is separated from his fellow prisoner by a partition so that he cannot see or speak to anyone. Hanging on to a small handle at the end of a chain, the prisoner then commences to tread the wheel, all the weight of his body falling upon the treads, which were small and close, with only enough room for the toes. Falls and injuries were common. The man would work for 16 minutes, and then rest for 8 throughout the allotted period. Officers patrolled above the wheel, and any man reported for any wrong-doing might lose a meal or be put on bread and water.

The 'crank' was another punishment, and was simply a handle fixed in the cell wall that the convict had to turn. Attached to it was an indicator of how much work the operator had done, while the attending officer could turn a screw to make the device easy or hard to turn. This is how prison officers came to be called 'Screws'. As mentioned earlier, oakum picking was another popular practice, and one pound of oakum was handed out to be picked and then weighed again after finishing. Oakum was the cast-off remains of tarred ships' ropes, from an inch upward in thickness, and it had to be picked with the bare fingers until it was as fine as hair. At first the work is hard on the fingers, which quickly become sore, but with continued use, the fingers

Corner Tower of Stafford Prison at the time of the trial of the three boatmen.

become hardened to the process, so that an old hand can pick as much oakum in an hour as a new man in six.

Those who may be regarded as the favoured prisoners were tailors, shoemakers, painters and bricklayers, for they were able to follow their trade inside. They are soon put to their trades, so that prison was no more than confinement, except of course that they must be in silence; but even there, some prisoners learned to talk to another without moving their lips. Otherwise the wards and corridors were as silent as the grave. In addition to those occupations mentioned, there was a mat factory, a basket factory, a laundry and, of course, a kitchen, and to work in that was the most prized occupation of all.

CHAPTER 8

The Rape and Murder of Christina Collins on the Trent & Mersey Canal, Second Trial

Before Mr Baron Gurney. 1840
Conviction of the Three Boatmen

The avenues leading to the court were early crowded with persons anxious to hear the trial of the Boatmen for murder which had been fixed to come on this morning. Mr Baron Gurney had however, strictly forbidden the admission of many persons, and the court itself was consequently not so full as we have been accustomed to see it. The case however excited the utmost degree of interest, and there was an extraordinary number of gentlemen of the bar in court during the trial.

James Owen, aged 39; George Thomas, alias Dobell, aged 27; and William Ellis, alias Lambert, aged 23, were placed at the bar on the charge of the wilful murder of Christina Collins, the wife of Robert Collins, on the 17th of June last, at the Parish of Rugeley – by 'casting, pushing or throwing the said Christina Collins into the canal' by which means 'the said Christina Collins was suffocated, choked and drowned'. The prisoners were also charged with the same offence under the Coroner's Inquisition.

The prisoners having severally pleaded **NOT GUILTY**, a respectable and intelligent jury (of which Mr Edward Walley of Hanley in the Potteries was foremost) was sworn well and truly in to try, and a true deliverance to make between our Sovereign Lady the Queen and the prisoners at the bar, and a true verdict to give according to the evidence.

These men, it was recollected were tried at the last Summer Assizes, before Mr Justice Williams, on an indictment charging them of committing a rape upon the body of Christina Collins. After a long investigation, and the case for the prosecution having closed, the learned judge decided that although a strong case of suspicion had been raised against the prisoners, yet there was no legal evidence of any rape having been committed by them, and directed the jury to acquit the prisoners, which they accordingly did. Mr Sergeant Ludlow then applied to the court to put off the trial, under the indictment for murder, until these Assizes, under the ground that a material witness, Joseph Orgill, a prisoner in the gaol who had been convicted of bigamy, could not be examined in the case until he had obtained a free pardon through an application to the Secretary of State. Owen, it was understood, had made important disclosures to Orgill whilst in prison. The counsel for the prisoners opposed the application, but Mr Justice Williams consented to postpone the trial.

On the present occasion, the men had much the same appearance when placed at the bar as at the last Assizes. They had on the sleeve waistcoats usually worn by boatmen.

Mr Sergeant Ludlow opened the case, he said – the prisoners at the bar had been arraigned on the inquisition of the Coroner, and also on indictment found by the grand jury at the last summer Assizes on the charge of the wilful murder of Christina, the wife of Robert Collins, and they had pleaded 'not guilty' and for their trial had put themselves on the jury and their country; and they (the jury) had to enter upon a very important and anxious enquiry; an enquiry into the circumstances by which a fellow creature had lost her life, and might involve the prisoners at the bar in the punishment of death. He need say nothing more than that to secure their anxious attention to the facts which would be proved in evidence. It was impossible that an event like this could have happened without being the subject of much general conversation; and the jury might have received impressions unfavourable to the prisoners out of court from a previous acquaintance with the particulars of the charge against them.

The prisoners had a right to expect a fair, deliberate and unbiased consideration of those circumstances only which would be proved in evidence that day, and he besought them to dismiss from their minds everything which would prevent them from giving an unprejudiced decision. They would have the able assistance of the learned judge who presided in coming to that decision; and if after investigating the facts of this case they entertained any reasonable doubt, either upon the facts themselves, or the inferences to be drawn from those facts, the prisoners were entitled to a verdict of acquittal. If on the other hand, they should be satisfied from those facts that the deceased came to her death by the means and through the instrumentality of the persons specified in the indictment, it would be their duty to find them guilty.

He would now lay before them a short simple and naked statement of the circumstances of this melancholy case. They were circumstances which could not be heard without exciting strong feelings with regard to the unfortunate woman who had lost her life. The deceased, Christina Collins, was the wife of Robert Collins. They were both in a humble situation in life. She had been employed in Liverpool for some months, assisting in the dress making business; and her husband had been unable to procure any employment, and was dependant on his wife. In the latter end of May last, he left Liverpool to go to London, to endeavour to find a situation; and being successful, he took an early opportunity of sending a sovereign to his wife for the purpose of enabling her to join him in London.

She accordingly took her passage in a barge from Liverpool on Saturday the 15th of June, and on arriving at Preston Brook, was forwarded as passenger in one of Pickford and Company's canal boats, of which the prisoner Owen was captain, and two of the other prisoners, and a boy of the name Musson, were the crew. She had two boxes and a bundle with her. The learned Sergeant then observed that nothing worth notice occurred until the arrival of the boat at Stoke upon Trent, at noon, when some conversation took place between one of the prisoners and the deceased, which was the first important point in the case. He would here remark that part of the cargo of the boat consisted of spirits, and he believed that these men had made free with it, and had by those means lost part of their usual restraint over themselves, which he feared was at the very best feeble.

The learned Sergeant then traced the progress of the boat to Stone, where the prisoners were observed to be intoxicated, and where the deceased complained of their condition, and expressed fears that she should be ill treated by them. Then again near Sandon, a fellow boatman would prove that two of the prisoners made disgusting allusions to the deceased, one of them threatening what he would do. It would then be proved that at the Hoo Mill lock, the lock keeper's wife was disturbed in bed by cries of distress, and on getting up and going to the window, she observed a boat of Pickford's and three men. She saw also a female who was crying, and she heard her say

Brindley Bank pumping station.

'Don't attempt me; I'll not go down.' She enquired of the boatmen who she was, and they said 'A passenger.' And in reply to a further enquiry, said her husband was with her, which was not the fact. That was about midnight. At five o'clock in the morning, the body of the unfortunate woman was found in the canal at Brindley's Bank, about a mile this side of Rugeley. The learned Sergeant stated the particulars respecting the conduct of the prisoners after the boat passed Brindley's bank; which will appear in the evidence.

He then concluded by observing that the deceased might have fallen into the water accidently; she might have thrown herself in, in a state of excitement, or she might have been thrown in by the three prisoners, or some one of them. By which of these means she came to her death, they would have to judge from the evidence of the witnesses who would be called before them. Of one thing he was quite sure, whatever turn this case might take, they would have the benefit of its having been presented to them in the most clear and lucid manner by the learned judge, than whom no man was better able to discharge that important duty. Whatever the result might be, he felt convinced that the justice of the country would be fully satisfied. He repeated that if they should be of the opinion that there was so much reasonable doubt as to leave their minds in a state of uncertainty as to the mode and instruments of the death of this unfortunate woman, the prisoners were entitled to an acquittal; if not, they were bound to find them guilty. The learned counsel then proceeded to call the witnesses.

William Brookes – In June last, I was living at Stoke upon Trent; I was a porter at Messrs Pickford's establishment. On Sunday the 16th of June a boat arrived at about 12 o'clock noon on its way to London. It remained at Stoke about four hours; James Owen had the command of that boat. Thomas, Ellis and the boy Musson were the

Christina Collins' grave and Rugeley Church.

crew. There was a woman passenger with the boat. The woman said something. (Mr Godson objected to anything being stated affecting any prisoner unless he was in hearing.) In consequence of something she said, I gave her some directions what to do. I saw Thomas; he said something to her, but what I could not hear. I heard her say to Thomas 'Leave me alone. I'll not have anything to say to you.'

Hugh Cordwell – I am check clerk for the Trent and Mersey Canal Company at Stone. I saw the dead body of a woman at Rugeley on Tuesday the 18th of June last. I had seen that woman before alive on Sunday the 16th of June. She was with a boat under the command of the prisoner Owen which arrived at Stone about eight o'clock in the evening; she was tying up a bundle in the boat and was about getting out when I told her not to do so until I had gauged the boat. After I had gauged the boat the woman got out and she said –

    Mr Baron Gurney – Did the prisoners hear what she said?

    Cordwell – No.

    Mr Baron Gurney – Then if it was anything affecting them, you must not repeat it. (To Mr Sergeant Ludlow – You may enquire generally whether she remarked upon the condition of the men.)

    Cordwell continued – She remarked upon the condition that the crew were in. I had observed what condition they were in. They were all in liquor – Owen in particular. She got out of the boat and walked against the battlements of the bridge. Owen went to her and asked her why she did not follow him through the town? I did not hear her reply. She then walked on under the canal bridge going away from Owen. She did not give any drink to the men, nor did she take any. The two other prisoners were with the boat. There was no other boat of Pickford's in the same direction until half past eleven that night. Owen's boat left Stone at 10 minutes past eight.

Thomas Bloor – I was captain of a boat called *The Emma*, and was passing with it between Fradley and Stone on Sunday the 16th of June; I was going toward Liverpool. There was another boat – Gleddy's in company of mine. I met another boat – one of Pickford's nearer Sandon than Aston lock, just as it was getting dusk at night. I saw Owen on board that boat. Something passed between me and Owen. Thomas came onto our boat for a glass of ale. I saw a woman on Owen's boat. Owen pointed to the woman and said 'Will you have anything of this?' I said 'No – I have no inclination.' Thomas said Jemmy had had concerns with her that night, and he would, or else he would 'burke her'.

Bloor – Cross-examined by Mr Godson – I had been drinking; there had been wakes where our boat had passed. We had a gallon amongst five of us – I was sober. It was about four miles I think from Haywood where we met Owen's boat. We had had no ale for three days until we came to Haywood. I was examined at the last Assizes. I think he said something about 'burking' on that occasion. I am certain he said it; I will swear he said it.

Robert Walker – I had the command of a boat on the Sunday evening, the 16th June last. I remember meeting a woman on the towing path that evening near Salt Bridge. I spoke to her; she gave me no answer. I afterwards met one of Pickford's boats. I was asked by one of the men with the boat whether I had met a passenger of theirs. I said 'yes.' He said – 'How far is she before?' I said 'Not far.' One made answer – he said 'he wanted to — her.'

By the Judge – Was that said loud enough to be heard by other men in Pickford's boat?

Bloor – I cannot tell. I cannot tell who the man was who said that.

Ann Mills – I am the wife of James Mills, the lock keeper at the Hoo Mill lock. On Saturday night on the 16th of June last, I heard a noise at the lock – a cry. I thought as if somebody was abusing a child, a cry of distress; I got up and opened the window. A boat of Pickford's was in the lock. A woman was sitting on the cabin; she got off the top of the cabin. She cried out she had lost her shoe; after she had stooped down, as if putting her shoes on, I saw her at the top of the cabin again with her legs hanging on the outside. There were three men with the boat. She said – 'Don't attempt me – I'll not go down – I'll not go in there.' The man on the lock side said 'mind her legs' which were hanging outside. I called to the man under the window and asked 'what woman that was they had with them?' He said 'A passenger.' I asked if she had anyone with her. And he said 'Her husband.'

Cross-examined – I know it was Pickford's boat by the letter board; they are large white letters, different from the other boats.

Mr Godson – Did you ask whether the woman had anybody with her, or whether she had anyone belonging to her?

Mills – Anybody with her.

Mr Baron Gurney – It does not signify which. It means the same thing.

Mr Godson – Not exactly my Lord.

By the Judge – It is nine miles from our lock to Stone.

The judge to the jury – Gentlemen you'll remember that Owen's boat left Stone at ten minutes past eight o'clock; and Cordwell said no other boat of Pickford's went in that direction until half past eleven at night, and Owen's boat had got nine miles from Stone at this time.

James Mills – I keep the Hoo Mill lock. I remember on Sunday the 16th of June last, hearing a scream in the night; a cry as if of distress. This was about 12 o'clock at night. I got up and looked over my wife's shoulder through the window and saw a woman on the top of the cabin of the boat.

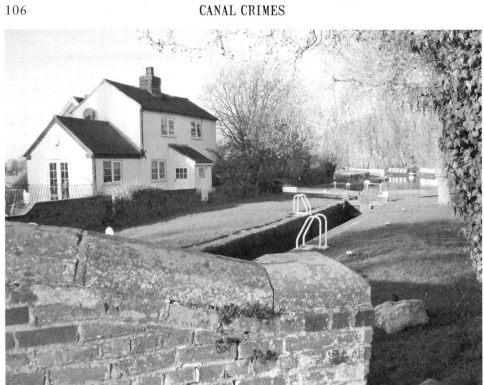

Hoo Mill Lock, looking north.

Hoo Mill Lock, looking south.

By the Judge – My wife made some enquiry of the boatmen respecting the woman. She asked what woman they had with her. They said 'A passenger'. She asked whether she had anybody with her, belonging to her. They said she had – 'Her husband.'

William Hatton – In June last I belonged to a boat of Messrs Bache and Co. I know a place on the canal called Brindley's Bank. There used to be a watering place between Brindley's Bank and Rugeley. I was at that place between one and two o'clock that morning. I came up with a boat of Pickford's between the watering place and the stop place at Brindley's Bank. I saw Thomas and Owen on the bank. They asked me if I had seen a woman. I said no I had not. They asked me again if I had seen one. I said I had not. They asked me if I had seen one between here and Turnover Bridge. I said no I had not. They then turned back from me and spoke amongst themselves. I was going the same way as their boat. My boat had not gone before theirs then, but it did so soon afterwards. This boat of Pickford's was the first of Pickford's boats that I had overtaken that night. This place was I should think about three or four miles from Hoo Mill lock. I got up to Owen's boat at Rugeley wharf, about a mile further.

Cross-examined – The stop place is a stone's throw from Brindley's Bank. At Brindley's Bank the canal takes a very sharp turn toward Rugeley. The fly boats travel about three miles an hour. The canal is generally about 40 feet wide, or the width of four or five boats. It is shallow by places towards the banks; the deep water is only about the width of two boats. At Brindley's Bank, the current of the water is toward London. It is nearly a mile from Brindley's Bank to Rugeley wharf. I was at the horse's head of my boat when I met Owen and Thomas. It was not light enough for me to see them at any distance. When I could see them, their faces were toward me, and they were as if coming from the direction of Rugeley. Judging from the rate at which boats travel, I should think that Owen's boat was at Rugeley wharf at that time.

Saturn – one of the last fly-boats on Britain's canals.

By the Judge – I had come through the aqueduct at that time.

William Lowe – On Monday morning the 17th of June, I was steering a boat near Rugeley Church; I was going toward Stoke. Beyond Rugeley Church, I met a boat of Pickford's. There was no driver with the horse; I saw a person steering the boat. I then met Bache's boat. There was a man talking to the driver of Bache's boat. Two other men were following, going the same road; one of the two men was without a coat.

James Willday – I was the captain of one of Bache's boats on the morning of Monday the 17th of June last. We had a kicking mare. When near Handsacre between three and four o'clock in the morning, I saw one of Pickford's boats. I saw James Owen jump off the middle plank end of that boat and stand against the bridge wall till the stern end came to him. Musson was steering Owen's boat. I spoke to Musson – I said – 'Hello my lad, tell your master to look out.' Upon that Musson put his head in the cabin and turned himself round and closed the doors. My boat was passing Owen's boat at that time. If the door's had not been closed I should have seen into the cabin.

Cross-examined – I am well acquainted with the canal; there is a sharp turn in the canal at Brindley's Bank. It is like an elbow. A person sitting on a boat would very likely be thrown off at that turn. The boat would tumble on one side – that is what we call a 'drop' or lurch. Even boatmen are liable to be thrown off when a boat lurches. I have been thrown off several times. I know the stop place near Brindley's Bank. From the stop place to the watering place is about five hundred yards. The current of the canal is toward London. There is a pretty strong current for a canal, but you cannot perceive the water flow. A cork would move, but not so as to be observed to move. It is what we call a 'ten mile pound' at that part of the canal. It is 10 miles from Colwich Lock to Woodend Lock. Brindley's Bank is about 3 miles from Colwich lock.

Re-examined – I never knew a single instance of a person being thrown off a boat at the sharp turn at Brindley's Bank. I have myself found it difficult to keep my standing in turning at that corner. It requires some care and attention in managing the boat.

William Musson – (This boy it will be recollected was one of the crew of the boat on the morning in question. He was at one time in custody on the same charge as the three prisoners.) I was one of the four persons employed in navigating one of Pickford's boats on Monday morning the 17th of June last. The prisoners at the bar were the other three. I got out of the boat at Colwich lock to go to the horse; the woman was on the bed place in the cabin when I left the boat at Colwich lock. Her bonnet and shoes were off; she had the rest of her clothes on. I got into the boat again at Brindley's Bank. The woman was not then in the boat. Owen was steering at that time and Thomas stood on the foot board.

By the Judge – At that time we had come round the turn about 40 yards.

Witness continued – We went around the turn the same as usual. I asked where the woman was. Owen said he believed she was drowned.

By the Judge – He did not say how lately he had seen her?

Witness continued – No. Owen asked me to lend him six shillings to pay Thomas. At Armitage Tunnel I wanted to get off, and told Owen who was in the middle of the boat to come. I got out of the cabin and went to the passengers place. One of the boxes belonging to the woman was opened; the lid was back. The box had been corded up with a light cord. I remember one of the captains of one of Bache's boats telling me to look out. Ellis, Thomas and Owen were then in the cabin. Ellis and Thomas were asleep. Owen told me to shut the doors; this was after we had passed Rugeley. I was confined in gaol at the same time, and in the same place as Ellis and Thomas. I did not hear either of them say anything about the woman; I am sure I did not.

Cross-examined – I saw the woman last at Colwich lock, when I got out of the boat to drive. The boat was at the stop place when I got on again. When the woman was missing, they did not attempt to stop the horse. They attempted to stop the horse about a mile or three quarters of a mile from Brindley's Bank. The boat was going on at the time I got on. Owen wanted six shilling off me to pay Thomas who was going to leave. The place for the passenger is in the middle of the boat. If the passenger was in that place, the person steering the boat would not see her, unless she was looking out. There were blankets put into the hole for the accommodation of the woman; they were put there on the Sunday night. I saw the woman lying down in the cabin with her shoes, bonnet and shawl off. Owen and I were lying down in the cabin at the same time.

Re-examined – I don't know how it happened that she was in the cabin. I did not see her coming into the cabin. I stayed about half an hour with the boat at Rugeley wharf.

In reply to a question put by the learned Judge from Mr Godson, the witness said that Ellis was asleep at Brindley's Bank.

In reply to another question put by the learned Judge at the request of Sergeant Ludlow, the witness said he knew that because he heard him snore.

By the Judge – A boat went by near Rugeley wharf when they were gone to look for the woman. Owen and Thomas got out at Rugeley; not before. When I saw the woman last, she was on the cross bed in the cabin, not in the passenger's place, and that was at Colwich lock. I remember being with Thomas at Aston lock, that was about seven or eight o'clock at night. Thomas said he wished the woman had been 'In hell, or somewhere – for he hated the sight of her.'

Mr Sergeant Ludlow further requested his Lordship to ask the witness what passed at Hoo Mill lock. The witness replied that he was in bed and asleep at the time, and did not hear any cry or noise whatever.

John Bladen – I am Wharfinger at Rugeley wharf. Rugeley lies between Brindley's Bank and Fazeley. In the course of the voyage up to London, Pickford and Company's boats stop there. On Monday morning the 17th of June, neither of the prisoners called to give any information about any passenger having been lost. I have been to the place where the body was found. There is a high bank there on the opposite side to the towing path. It is from 10 to 15 feet from the top of the bank to the surface water. The width of the canal is about 34 feet. The deepest water is from three feet nine to ten inches. It is that depth about two or three feet from the steep bank.

Ann Leigh – I am the wife of Jonathon Leigh, who keeps the Woodend lock. I remember on the morning of the 17th of June last, the prisoner Owen at the bar coming to our house about half past five o'clock. He said he was afraid that they had had a woman passenger drowned. I said I hope not. He said he was afraid they had. He could not tell what had become of her, for she was like she was deranged. She had been in the canal once up to the knees, and he fetched her out and put her into the cabin. Owen appeared to be all in a confusion at that time; he did not appear to be sober.

Cross-examined by Mr Godson – He appeared to be in confusion from liquor?

By the Judge – He trembled very much at the time. (Here one of the jury men turned to another, and by a very significant gesture appeared to say 'I told you so'.) He said he thought the woman had gone for a little walk. He said he thought she must be deranged for she kept calling out – 'Collins – Collins – Collins.'

Charles Robotham – I lived at Fradley in June last, and was a clerk of Pickford and Co's. On Monday morning the 17th, the prisoner Owen came about six o'clock with a boat, which was going toward London. While the horses were changing he came to me. I was milking a cow. He said 'A very bad job had happened.' They had

had a passenger booked at Preston Brook, and he believed she had drowned herself. He said she had 'attempted it once before, and he had pulled her out.' I told him he ought have taken more care of her, and left her at the first place he came to. He said he thought 'she was off her head.' I asked him why he thought so. He said because she kept on crying out – 'Collins – Collins – Collins.' He said the last place he saw her was Colwich lock. He said she had left her shoes and bonnet in the cabin. He wished me to take the boxes out. I said it was useless taking the boxes out; for we should find out who she was. I went to look at the boxes, and Thomas said it would be useless taking them out, for she would follow. I then wished Owen to go back with me, to see if we could find her. He was not willing. I thought it right to go to Fazeley, and I gave some information to Mr Kirk. I arrived there before the boat. Mr Kirk sent for two policemen.

On the arrival of the boat at Fazeley, we both went and told the prisoners that they were wanted in the office, and must bring the road note with them. Mr Kirk enquired where the passenger was. Owen said that they last saw her at Colwich lock. He said she had treated them with some ale at Stone. He said the last time he saw anything of her, was her getting out of the boat at Colwich lock. I think that was after the other prisoners had been apprehended. That was in the office. I went with the constable into the cabin and searched the boat. We found her bonnet and shoes there. I asked Owen what brought the woman into the cabin? That was not the place for passengers. He said she had been in the biggest part of the way. The others said she had not. They would not have her in the cabin. I afterwards saw Thomas and Ellis, and they said the last they had seen of the woman was at Colwich lock. The two boxes were corded when I saw them with white cord. The bonnet appeared crushed in all forms, as though very much pressed.

Cross-examined – Owen said – I am innocent and burst out a-crying. That was in the evening in the public house. I won't say whether Owen said – 'She got out of the cabin, or she got out of the boat' at Colwich lock. Owen said the other men quarrelled with him for letting her be in the cabin.

By the Judge – At the time he burst out a-crying, I was passing through the room in the public house where he was in custody, at Fazeley in the evening of Monday. He took me to the back door and said he was innocent, and said he hoped I would do what I could for him. He said if others did not have him (Robotham) as a witness at the inquest, he (Owen) should. The boat was out of time about three quarters of an hour when I came to Fazeley. I mentioned that to him. I do not recollect that he accounted for that by telling me he had turned back to look for the woman.

William Kirk – In June last, I was agent for Pickford and Co at Fazeley. On Monday morning the 17th Mr Robotham came to me. In consequence of what he said, I sent for a constable. I remember the arrival of the boat. The first person I saw was Ellis; I told him to bring the papers from the boat, and come into the office; I wanted to speak to him. These were the first words that passed. He replied 'Damn and blast the woman; if she has drowned herself, I cannot help it.' According to my recollection, I saw Ellis before he had seen Mr Robotham. I afterwards gave him into custody. I enquired for Owen; they said he was in the cabin. I told him he must bring the papers into the office, I wanted him. He came into the office, Robotham was there. I told Owen I understood that he had lost a passenger, and unless he could account for her, I must keep him until she was found. He said 'It was a very bad job, and he was very sorry for it.' I then went down to the boat to look for her clothes. He said they had left the woman at Colwich lock. He said he was afraid she was going off her head. He said she has made an attempt to drown herself; they had pulled her out of the canal once; and when she came to Colwich lock she got out of the boat and said 'She would ride no further.' I remember Thomas coming into the office; He said 'I hope the b—r (or bloody w—e) is burning in hell.' I said 'You are a drunk and a fool', that was in the office.

Cross-examined – Thomas was very drunk at the time. With my experience of the habits and language of boatmen, some of them use such as language as Thomas in their common talk.

The Judge said he could not refrain from remarking that he was afraid no men in this country were so destitute of all moral culture as boatmen. They were continually wandering about; they knew no Sabbath, and possessed no means of religious instruction.

Witness cross-examination continued – Thomas said 'if she had drowned herself, he could not help it.' He did not say – He was afraid she was drowned. Owen said – He was afraid she was drowned.

William Harrison – In June last, I was headborough in Fazeley. I was applied to by Mr Kirk, on Monday morning the 17th and went down to the canal side. I was there when Owen's boat arrived. Ellis said 'Damn and blast the woman. What do we know about the woman? If she had a mind to drown herself she might. Nobody had then asked him anything about the woman. This was after they had landed. Thomas and Ellis appeared to be drunk. Owen said 'he did not know what had become of the woman except her'd drowned herself.' I afterwards went to the cabin, and found the bonnet and shoes of the woman. They are much in the same state now as when I found them. Nothing has been done to alter the condition of the bonnet. (The bonnet was produced; the strings had not been untied, and the bonnet was quite altogether out of shape and pressed together.) When at Rugeley afterwards, Owen and I had some conversation about the place where the body was found, and Owen said 'She wanted very little drowning.' This was nearly a week after they were apprehended. I had been to look at the place, and I told Owen where I had been, and he said what I have already stated. I said I should think none at all. The water appeared to be not more than 18 or 19 inches deep.

Cross-examined – I had not been talking with regard to other kinds of violence. I mentioned at the last trial that Owen said 'She wanted very little drowning.'

Francis Jackson – I recollect being present when Owen was in custody at Fazeley on the 17th of June; I was handcuffed to him. A person whose name I do not recollect came to Owen. Owen said to him 'Go and tell those two men to be sure to swear that we left the woman at Colwich lock.' The same man came again next morning, and Owen enquired 'Have you told those men?' He replied 'I have.' Owen then said 'Go and tell them again and be sure.'

Mr Sergeant Ludlow said he now proposed to put in the depositions of the prisoners before the Coroner.

Mr Baron Gurney understood the examination of the prisoners before the Coroner had been upon oath. That being the case, they could not be received, or it would be bringing forward the evidence of prisoners against themselves.

Mr Godson – The point was mentioned on the trial at the last Assizes; and Mr Justice Williams gave his opinion against receiving them, because if he had, he (Mr Sergeant Ludlow) should not have pressed to have them read: It was contrary to his practice.

Mr Baron Gurney – If a matter were doubtful, and the evidence pressed, the judge would receive it no doubt, reserving the point; because in no other manner could the opinion of the judges be taken. In civil cases it was different. A new trial could be moved for. In criminal cases the evidence must be received, and the point reserved. He was not aware of any case in which evidence upon oath by the accused party had been received on a Coroner's Inquisition; but such evidence given before Magistrates had been tendered, and was uniformly rejected.

Mr Sergeant Ludlow referred to a case in which a magistrate had, in the first place, taken the deposition of a prisoner upon oath, but on discovering his mistake, the deposition was destroyed, and the examination taken in the usual way. But he left himself entirely in his Lordship's hands.

Mr Godson quoted 'The King v Wheeley' in Carrington and Payne's Reparis, in which the examination of a prisoner was rejected because it purported to be upon oath. He had quoted that case on the trial at Worcester of a man for the murder of his own wife. The man had originally been called to give evidence against another party, but the man himself being subsequently charged with the crime, he (Mr Godson) objected to his evidence being received against himself: and it was not received.

Mr Baron Gurney – If it was a point on which I entertained any doubt I would receive it, and reserve the point, but I have no doubt whatever that these depositions cannot be read.

Mr Sergeant Ludlow thought that in one instance, the oath had not been administered, and in that case perhaps his Lordship would allow it to be put in; but on examining the paper, it was found to be headed – 'James Owen upon oath saith.' Etc.

The depositions by the prisoners taken before the Coroner were consequently all rejected.

Thomas Brandt – I am a boatman; on the 17th of June last, I was on the line of canal near Brindley's Bank about 5 o'clock in the morning. I saw something in the water. It turned out to be the body of a woman; it was below Brindley's Bank about 80 yards from the stop place. It was about four feet from the side, on the side opposite the towing path, and where the water was about 18 or 19 inches deep. The bank on that side is about seven or eight yards high. A man of the name John Johnson assisted me in getting the body out of the water. She had no bonnet or shoes on; the face was downwards.

John Johnson – On the morning of the 17th of June, Brandt, the last witness called to me to assist him in getting something out of the canal; it was the body of a woman. It was about four feet from the bank of the canal, and the depth of the water was about 18 inches. The bank above is a high one; the face lay downwards. The body lay a little sloping; the body was warm; the water was rather warm. The place where it was found was about eighty yards below the stop place. I took the body to the Talbot at Rugeley.

Hannah Philips – I lived at Rugeley in June last. I remember an inquest being held in the month of June on the body of a woman; I saw the dead body of that woman; she had a gown on; a handkerchief about her neck, a white petticoat and a pair of drawers. I noticed the condition of the gown sleeves; there was a rip on the back of the left arm of the gown, and the gown body was a little torn. The neck handkerchief was also torn on the left shoulder.

Cross-examined – I was a witness when these men were charged with the rape and gave the same testimony.

Elizabeth Matthews – I assisted the last witness in taking off the clothes of the deceased. I took off the drawers, I produced them. They are in the same state as when I took them off. They are torn on the front, they are made of fine calico.

(The drawers were shown to the jury – they were rent completely across in front.)

Cross-examined – I appeared at the last Assizes, and gave the same evidence, when the prisoners were charged with the rape.

Elizabeth Grice – I am a dressmaker residing at Liverpool. I remember Christina

Collins leaving Liverpool on the 15th of June last. I observed her dress; no part of her dress or gown was torn; she was very neat in her person; I had known her about six months. She was a dressmaker by business and had assisted me.

Robert Collins, the husband of the deceased was then placed in the box (he was in a less excited state than when he appeared in the witness box at the last Assizes). Tears stood in his eyes during his short examination, and he shook his head expressively at the prisoners as he retired from the court. He said 'Christina Collins was my wife; I had left her in Liverpool about the latter end of May last. I afterwards sent her a sovereign to come up to me in London. I saw the body at the inquest at Rugeley; it was that of my wife.'

Mr Sergeant said the next witness was the one with respect to whom the trial was put off at the last Assizes. He did not know exactly what that witness would prove, but he thought it right to put him in the box.

Joseph Orgill – I was convicted at the last Assizes of bigamy, and have since received a pardon. While I was in gaol before my trial, Owen had a conversation with me. The conversation took place on the Sunday night during the Assizes. After we were locked up in the cell, we were talking about the trials. I said 'mine is a bad job.' He said 'So is mine.' He said 'I can't think why they have taken the boy away from the other two men. Perhaps he will be a witness against us. If he is going to be a witness against us, it is for other things, not for the woman. He did not know anything about her; the other two committed the rape upon her, and mauled her to death, but he was free from her. He said 'I'm afraid it will be a hanging job.' He trembled very much. He said 'I will tell you about it.'

We had been to Stoke, loading and unloading our boat. The woman was bound as a passenger for London; when they had done, she was in the cabin all the time to Stone; they had got some whiskey in the boat; they got some out and all drank of it; till they were drunk with the exception of the woman. She drank two or three times out of the cup; when they were drunk they began to be rough with the woman. She got out and walked on the towing path till she got out of sight; they went till they met a man whom they asked of a woman was before, he said there was. He said – 'she is a passenger of ours, and he wanted to — her.' When they got to the lock house, she was talking to a woman, saying they were getting drunk, and she was afraid they would molest her; she said she was afraid to go with them, but she did go. Dobell and Lambert ought to have been in bed at the time. When they went on from the lock, Dobell and Lambert got out of the boat and went along the tow path along with the woman and kept mauling her all the way. When they came near the next house, they committed a rape or rapes upon the woman. The woman had a pair of trowsers on. One held her while the other got a knife out of his pocket, and cut the trowsers out of the way; the woman screamed out; whether they heard her at the house he could not say; he supposed they were gone to bed. There might be twenty boats passing in the night; they got the woman in the boat again; it was then his turn and the boys to go to bed; the boy and he went to bed; the woman was in bed. He tried to have to do with her but he could not.

By the Judge – He did not say the reason?

Orgill – The woman said to him 'Oh captain, Oh captain, what shall I do? Oh my Collins, my Collins, I wish he was here.' They were in bed till they came to Colwich lock, when it was his turn and the boys to go to work, and the others to go to bed. Being drunk with the whiskey – or one thing and another, he was loathe to get up, but he did get up, the boy went to drive the horse, he steered the boat; the other two were in the cabin, and the woman. They got the bottle to have some more whiskey, and while they were having it, the woman slipped out of the cabin into the hatches, where he was; she made an attempt to get out of the boat, and got her legs half way

Approaching Fradley from Wood End.

in the water; he leaned over and pulled her out. They pulled her into the cabin again, where they committed rape or rapes upon her, and completely mauled her to death. I asked him if she was dead, and he said she was completely mauled to death. What made them do it was, they knew what they had been doing with her, and she would tell. When it was done, a quarrel arose among them about the woman. Dobell came out of the cabin to steer the boat, whilst he went in, and he took the woman out of the cabin, and laid her on top of the cabin. He went into the cabin again and was in some time. When he came out of the cabin again, the woman was gone; and whether Dobell pushed her off at the turn, or whether she rolled off by the swaying of the boat, or whether he pushed her off after they had got round the turn, he could not tell. Dobell knew the last of her. They had made a bad job of it, for they had left her shoes and bonnet in the cabin. It was about half a mile from Colwich lock where the woman was put on the cabin, but he could not tell exactly where Dobell pushed her off. I asked him what time it was, he said – 'Between one and two o'clock in the morning.' He said nothing more occurred until they came to Fradley Junction, to Mr Robotham's, where they wanted to leave the woman's things, but he objected.

He said Dobell and Lambert went to the place where the boxes were, and out of the box they took a piece of cotton print. He went to them and said they must leave the boxes alone, they should be in enough trouble without the boxes; the answer was – they should all be right about the woman if he held his noise, for nobody ever saw them do anything to her. They said – as to the boxes, she would come no more after them. He said – 'Did you take notice of that chapter that the parson read the Sunday before?' I asked him for what reason. Because he said 'it was a picked one for a purpose for us.' I said what makes you think so? He said 'Because there was so much about hanging in it.' He said 'I hope we shall not be hung; that we shall get off for transportation; and then I don't care. We have made a bad job of it altogether. If we had stopped the boat at Rugeley, and made an alarm to the people there, and had taken the people back, they would have had no suspicion; or even if we had taken the woman and left her in the middle of the boat in the place for passengers, nobody could have sworn we had done it, and Pickford's would have been fined a sovereign for not finding straw. If Dobell and Lambert had gone to bed at Colwich lock, and left her alone after we had gone through Colwich lock, she would have been alive and well enough.

Orgill was very respectably dressed; he gave his evidence in a clear and straightforward manner, without any hesitations.

Cross-examined by Mr Godson – Orgill – I have not the same dress on that I had the other day when I left the gaol. I had a smock frock on then. I am a butcher by trade; I was indicted for bigamy at the last Assizes. I am a married man with four children; I had left my wife and family in England, and gone to Ireland where I lived five or six weeks with the second person I married. I cannot say whether I left her in the family way. I was tried on the Monday or Tuesday after this conversation took place; I believed these men were tried on the same day, or the day following; I was down below during the time of their trial. I cannot say how long it was after I had received the judgment of the judge that I said a word about what Owen had been saying to me. I said it for the first time while I was below. I heard they were on their trial. It might be an hour or more after I had received my own judgment that I mentioned this; I was not told at that moment that I should have a pardon. I did not hear anything of a pardon until I came into court the other day to receive it; I can read and write. I did not know whether a pardon would be necessary before I could become a witness. I had no thought of giving evidence at all when I first mentioned it. I was not asked to make an affidavit. It was only about a fortnight or three weeks before the last sessions but one that what I had to say was taken down; I did not at the last Assizes give them any evidence. I told then a few words; the few words were that Owen had told me she was dead before she was put in the water; Owen told me so; that was the chief substance. I was examined a fortnight before the last sessions but one for the first time. I told the same story now that I did then. I have never varied from the long story that I have been telling you; I told all that I have now told. The lawyer for the prosecution took it down. He wrote it as I said it. I did not know before Owen told me for what he was in gaol. Owen knew some of my relations, but I did not know Owen. We used to lie awake for an hour talking; He had talked about it before, but he told me the whole of the case that night. I have been along the canal in some parts. I don't know Brindley's Bank. I don't know Colwich Lock. I was let out of custody on Friday night. I have been at Rugeley since. I have not been on the banks of the canal since. I have not been nearer the canal than the turnpike road; the canal runs by Rugeley. I never heard anything about the pardon at the last Assizes. I had not robbed my second wife. I had not taken her money. I did not get any property by her; I had a watch of hers; she gave it to me in Ireland. She followed me to England, and I gave it to her again.

The witness **Johnson** was recalled; he said that when the body was taken out of the water, there was a little froth at the mouth.

Mr Samuel Barnet – Surgeon, Rugeley, was examined. I examined the body of the woman upon whom an inquest was held at Rugeley in June last. I observed two small bruises below the elbow and the wrist of the right arm. I opened the body and examined its internal state; there was froth in the mouth and throat. I found the cavities on the right side of the heart gorged with blood, also the vessels leading to the lungs; the general viscera were perfectly healthy. There was from half a pint to a pint of water in the stomach; the bronchia were filled with frothy mucus.

Mr Sergeant Ludlow – Mr Barnet, I know you will excuse me asking the question – have you been regularly educated as a surgeon?

Barnet – I have, and I have had twenty-one years of experience in the profession at Rugeley.

Mr Ludlow – Are you able to say from the appearances you observed what the cause was of that woman's death?

Barnet – I conceive death was occasioned by suffocation from drowning. I form my judgment from the appearances I observed.

Mr Ludlow – Supposing the body had been thrown into the water dead, would those appearances have presented themselves?

Barnet – Not unless the body had been immersed in the water for a length of time.

Cross-examined by Mr Yardley – **Barnet** – I never examined more than two bodies of persons who had died of drowning before this. I did not open the head. If I had done so, I should most likely have found all the vessels surcharged with blood; the appearances in the head would have been the same if the death was from suffocation, whether it was from drowning or not. If the body had been immersed for a considerable time, water might have found its way into the stomach; if death had taken place before the immersion, that would have been the effect of the relaxation of the muscles. The frothy mucus is occasioned by the air in the windpipe meeting the water and occasioning a gurgling. The symptoms of death by drowning are not always decisive; they are sometimes uncertain.

Mr Sergeant Ludlow – That is the case for the prosecution my Lord.

Mr Godson said that in the indictment, the means of death must be described, and the evidence must meet that description. Now he begged to submit without argument, which was not allowed, that there was no evidence that the prisoners, or either of them did, according to the terms of the indictment, cast, throw or push, the deceased into the water.

Mr Baron Gurney – That is a question for the jury.

Mr Godson then proceeded to address the jury in a long and able speech for the prisoners. He said they were called upon to perform a duty which as far as his knowledge went, had never before fallen to the lot of a British jury. They were trying three men for the second time, on precisely the same facts, excepting only the statement of Orgill, as those on which a jury had acquitted them at the last Assizes. It was one of the first principles of criminal justice that a man should not be put in jeopardy of his life for a second time on the same facts for two offences. The present prosecution, however, was an inquiry into precisely the same facts as those adduced on the former trial. The same attorney and the same eminent counsel were again engaged, and the same hand had no doubt drawn up each indictment. There had indeed been four indictments; one for rape, another for murder, a third for an assault and a fourth for robbery. He could bring on this occasion the evidence of the learned Sergeant against himself; for after he had put them on their trial for the rape, and the judge had decided that there was no evidence to go to the jury, the learned Sergeant suggested that at any rate they might be convicted – of what – did the jury think 'Of murder?' No such thing. Of an assault with an attempt to commit rape? No but of a common assault.

Mr Baron Gurney – We have nothing to do with what passed on a former occasion.

Mr Godson – The prisoners were now being tried on an indictment found at the last Assizes, on the same evidence, with the addition of the statement of Orgill. Now Orgill's statement must be taken into the case, or it must be rejected. The indictment alleged the cause of death to be drowning; now Orgill's statement went to show that the woman was not drowned. The question for the jury was – did the prisoners drown the woman? It was not whether she ceased to breathe under the baleful influence of their brutal embraces. The evidence must be considered in that view. He feared the jury would find it extremely difficult to divest their minds of prejudice against these men. They could not have failed to receive impressions unfavourable to them. They must have closed their eyes and shut their ears not to have seen accounts and heard reports of this tragic case. The evidence before the Coroner had been extensively promulgated, as also had the proceedings at the last Assizes, and observations had been made by anyone who pleased on this extraordinary case. Men read and heard with horror these exaggerated reports, so that it was next to impossible for anyone to come to the consideration of the facts without a decided leaning against the prisoners. He had perceived that the jury were not uninfluenced by such a leaning, from what had passed when the woman was questioned about whether Owen did not tremble.

He implored them therefore to guard themselves against themselves, for he knew from his own experience how likely it was to think that because these men appeared to have had something to do with the death of this unfortunate woman, they necessarily caused her death. The facts themselves, carefully considered, would not however warrant such a conclusion. The facts really implicating the prisoners were comprised in a very short compass. He would first of all consider them without Orgill's story, and then with it. They might be taken up at the time the boat was approaching Colwich lock, to the time they arrived at Brindley's Bank, and what did the evidence show? That Thomas and Ellis were asleep in the cabin; the captain steering and the boy driving the horse. The woman according to one statement, left the boat at Colwich lock, according to another – left the cabin, and as the latter was most favourable to the prisoners, he had a right according to the merciful rule of British law, to adopt that. How great the probability that on leaving the cabin to go to the passengers place, she was thrown off by the lurching of the boat. He begged the jury to remember that they must withdraw their minds from the consideration

Fradley in winter.

of any other violence which might have been perpetrated upon this woman. What told against them on the occasion of their former trial would tell in their favour now; because if their treatment, however brutal, induced her to throw herself into the water in a state of excitement, shame and remorse, or had weakened her to such a degree, that she fell in involuntarily, that was not a throwing and pushing into the canal by these men, which would accord with the terms of the indictment.

But there was evidence to carry the point in their favour still further. It was shown that they returned from Rugeley wharf to look for the woman, and that they expressed an opinion afterwards that she had drowned herself, or would follow them. Then with regard to Orgill's statement, they must take it altogether, or reject it altogether. If Orgill's evidence was true, it disproved that indictment; it went distinctly to show that the woman was dead before she left the boat. Orgill's evidence must not affect Thomas and Ellis, because the law wisely and humanely said that the statements of accused persons against their accomplices, made in their absence, should not be received against them. What however were the probabilities as to the truth of Orgill's story? He a married man with four children, had been convicted of deserting his first wife and marrying another. His very crime was the one of all others, which proved next to perjury and utter want of good faith. He had gone to the altar to pledge himself under the holiest sanction, to a confiding female, when at the same time he was incompetent to do so. Such a man was one whom they ought to be most disinclined to believe. The learned counsel commented on different parts of the evidence at considerable length, and concluded by entreating the jury to give the benefits of the doubts which must arise in their minds on the calm consideration of the circumstances. The evidence was far from satisfactory; indeed that of the surgeon would raise a doubt whether the woman was drowned at all; for he admitted that the symptoms of death by drowning were not always decisive. In this state of doubt was the case left, and he confidently expected that under such circumstances, the jury would acquit the prisoners.

Mr Baron Gurney – Then proceeded to sum up the evidence. He said he had never met with such a case in the whole course of his experience, which made a larger demand upon the patience, the attention and discrimination of a jury. The learned counsel who had just addressed them had very properly cautioned them against reports which must have been current throughout this country on this melancholy case. In this world we had no good which was wholly unmixed with evil. The benefits of a free press had its alloy. By the publicity given to reports and rumours, the minds of jurymen were no doubt liable to be influenced, and all that could be done, was most earnestly to entreat them to dismiss from their minds anything they might have heard or read, and to apply their minds to the evidence alone as it had been given on this occasion. The indictment charged the three prisoners with the wilful murder of Christina Collins, and it charged them with effecting that murder by drowning her; and before they could find a verdict of guilty, they must be fully satisfied that they threw her into the water, and that they effected her death in that way, and no other.

The first fact which had been given in evidence bearing on the case was applicable to Thomas. The witness proved that at Stoke, Thomas was speaking to the deceased; therefore something was said to her, in reply to which the witness heard her say – she would have nothing to do with him – The next witness proved that they arrived at Stone at about eight o'clock in the evening, and that the deceased was in the boat tying her bundle; she made some remark to the witness as to the condition of the crew, and he observed that they were in liquor. He would here observe that the identity of the boat in its progress had been placed beyond all doubt. The men at Stone had proved that the boat in question was the only one of Pickford's that had passed in that direction that night until half past eleven o'clock. Before he noticed the next fact, he would inform the jury that they must bear in mind particularly that what one man said of either of the others was not evidence against the other if he was not present, and near enough to hear. If it applied, it was evidence against himself, but against himself only. The next witness proved that Thomas had said – he would have something to do with the woman that night, or else he would Burke her. With respect to the evidence of the boy Musson, this observation applied. They must receive it with great caution. He had been confined in the gaol with the two prisoners, and they would not forget the particular instructions given by Owen to the others to say – that the woman had left the boat at Colwich lock. They would also recollect that he had denied hearing any cries of distress at Hoo Mill lock, when he said he was asleep in the cabin, although they had been loud enough to disturb the repose of the woman at the lock house. Without that of Orgill, the evidence amounted to this – that this woman is taken on board a boat navigated by three men and a boy, of which boat Owen is the captain, and the two men and the boy the crew, and that the dead body of that woman is found in the canal at five o'clock in the morning, warm.

Undoubtedly as a passenger she was under the care of the persons navigating that boat; and they naturally required her at the hands of those in whose custody she had been placed, and they had to look to their conduct and declarations before the time of her death, and also after it was ascertained that she was dead. In the first place there was a declaration on the part of Thomas – that he would have connection with her, and he would. At midnight, the scream of a woman was heard, and an entreaty not to 'Attempt her.' Then there was a question from the witness as to whether she had a protector, and the answer of one of the men, she had, her husband. That was the last time she was seen alive by anyone but the crew of the boat. After the boat passed Brindley's Bank, there were declarations by the men that she was missing, and then by the prisoner Owen that she had got out at Colwich lock. These were briefly the different facts on which they had to decide, independently of Orgill's statement, whether the prisoners had been the means of procuring the death of this woman.

The additional evidence was that of Orgill. He concurred with the learned counsel in the opinion that Orgill's evidence must be received with great jealousy, as proceeding from a witness tainted with crime; but it must be remembered at the same time that he was not tainted in regard to this particular transaction. The evidence of an accomplice in the greatest crime was received if corroborated. This was the evidence of a witness who had been tried and convicted of a serious offence, and must be received with jealousy and watchfulness. At the same time, they must give it due attention and judge from the statement itself, from the manner, demeanour and mode of the witness, whilst giving his evidence to what degree of credit he was entitled.

A good many observations had been made upon that man's evidence, not quite justified by the fact. The man was not speaking to facts of his own knowledge, but to a declaration made by Owen. He was not responsible for the truth of the statement made by Owen. What was said by Owen in that statement, affecting the others in their absence, was no evidence against the others; it was evidence against himself alone, and that not directly perhaps, but in comparison with his other declarations, shewing the difference between that account, and what he had said at other times.

His Lordship then proceeded to read Orgill's statement, and continued – if they took this to be a true account of the transaction of Owen, it would be seen excused himself from all participation either in the rape or murder, whilst he accused the other two of both rape and murder. He knew it would be a difficult task for them; but he again entreated them not to allow what Owen said in the absence of the others to weigh with them at all to their disadvantage. From the good sense they had shown in former cases, he had confidence that they would act with proper discrimination on this point.

If Owen spoke truly, they were all entitled to their acquittal under this indictment. When he made that statement, he was on the eve of trial, knowing that he was charged with rape, and with murder by drowning, and he told the story which had been repeated. The use to make of that declaration was not to ascertain whether it was all literally true, but to compare his account then with his conduct before and the declarations he had given before, and then to form their judgment from the disparity between the two. His Lordship in alluding to the evidence of the surgeon, said that there was no doubt that death was caused by suffocation, and the surgeon considered the suffocation by drowning. In many cases of circumstantial evidence the chain of circumstances was so complete, and the facts so decisive, that an opinion might be given with as much certainty as if positive evidence of the crime was adduced; but in others, as in this, a great deal of careful consideration was required; and it was the business of an intelligent jury to weigh well the whole circumstances, and not to suffer themselves to be misled by their feelings so as to come to a conclusion which might be erroneous. He would give them this further caution; that the conviction of crime was not the first object of British courts of justice. It was far better that guilty men should escape punishment, than that one man should suffer unjustly. They must take the whole of the evidence into their careful consideration, and if that convinced them that the three prisoners at the bar (and it was difficult to distinguish between them) were guilty of the murder of this woman by drowning her, and not by any other means, then they would find them guilty, but, if they entertained a fair and reasonable doubt that they did actually drown her, however they might feel disgusted at their conduct in other respects, and however great might be the suspicions which rested upon them, they would find them not guilty.

In conclusion, his Lordship observed that we should always take care that the disgust and abhorrence justly excited against the crime should not allow us to be satisfied with less but rather to require stronger proof of the accused parties being its perpetrators.

The jury asked permission of his Lordship to retire to consider their verdict. A bailiff was accordingly sworn in to attend them, and they retired to the clerk of the indictments room. After an absence of from half to three quarters of an hour, they returned into court, and their names having been called over, every person in court appeared to await with breathless anxiety their verdict. In reply to the usually questions from Mr Bellamy, the foreman replied that they were all agreed, and that they found the three prisoners guilty.

No visible alteration marked the countenance of the prisoners on the verdict being given, except for the moment Owen became a little paler.

SENTENCE OF DEATH PASSED UPON THE PRISONERS

After a short pause, and the black coif, emblematical of death, having been placed upon the judge's head.

Mr Bellamy enquired with much feeling, what the prisoners had to say why judgment of death should not be passed upon them? They made no remark.

The crier having made the usual proclamation for silence, Mr Baron Gurney addressed them as follows –

'James Owen, George Thomas and William Ellis – after a long and patient hearing of the circumstances of this case, and after due deliberation on the part of the jury, you have been found guilty of the foul crime of murder – murder committed on an unoffending and helpless woman who was under your protection, and who there is reason to believe, was first the object of your lust; and then to prevent detection for that crime was the object of your cruelty! Look not for pardon in this world – Apply to the God of mercy, for that pardon which he alone can extend to penitent sinners and prepare yourselves for the ignominious death that awaits you. The case is one of the most painful, the most disgusting and the most shocking that ever came under my knowledge; and it remains for me only to pass upon you the awful sentence of the law – That you be taken to the place from whence you came, and from thence to the place of execution, and that you, and each of you be hanged by the neck until you are dead; and that your bodies afterwards be buried within the precincts of the prison; and may God have mercy on your souls.'

The prisoners were wholly unmoved during the delivery of this awful sentence, although the learned judge himself was evidently so much affected as to be able with difficulty to proceed: and the most solemn feeling pervaded all present. The prisoners were then removed from the bar.

STAFFORDSHIRE ADVERTISER SATURDAY 11 APRIL 1840

In London, Queen Victoria holds a levee at St James's Palace. Her Majesty and Prince Albert and suite, escorted by a party of Life Guards arrived in four state carriages from Buckingham Palace. The queen was attended by the Duchess of Sutherland and other dignitaries. In her drawing room she held the first gathering of the season. Meanwhile in Paris, rioting has been reported in many parts of the country regarding the high price of food. Meanwhile, at Stafford gaol, our three prisoners await execution.

Mr Passman – Solicitor for the prisoners – Owen Thomas and Ellis, condemned to death at our late Assizes for murder, having obtained all the information he could collect on their behalf, laid it before the Hon and Rev A. C. Talbot, who with great disinterestedness and humanity went to London with it purposely on Monday last, and laid it before the Marquis of Normanby, the Secretary of State for the Home Department. We mentioned last week that one of the principle objects would be to invalidate the testimony of Orgill, and to show particularly that the case against Ellis was by no means strong. Mr Talbot had some conversation with Lord Normanby and left the papers with him, which his Lordship promised would have his most serious attention. Yesterday morning communications were received from his Lordship by the governor of the prison, and by Mr Passman, stating that the law must take its course. The letter to Mr Passman was then as follows –

Whitehall 9th of April 1840

Sir, I am directed by the Marquis of Normanby to acquaint you that he has given the most attentive consideration to the documents he has received on behalf of William Ellis, James Owen and George Thomas – three convicts under the sentence of death in Stafford gaol for murder, and to express to you his Lordship's regret that he can perceive no sufficient ground to justify him consistently with his public duty in recommending the prisoners to the mercy of the crown. The law will therefore take its course at the expiration of the respite, which was granted to afford time to make enquiries into the case.

I am Sir – your most humble and obedient servant – S. M. PHILLIPS

C. B. Passman Esq. Stafford

After the communications had been received, the governor of the prison – T. Brutton Esq., informed the culprits that not the slightest hope now existed of their being saved; indeed he had all along dissuaded them from cherishing any such expectation. During the forenoon, F. M. Twemlow Esq. the chairman of the quarter sessions, and G. Keen Esq., (Deputy under Sheriff) visited the prison, and saw the culprits, as also did F. V. Lee Esq. and M. Gaunt Esq., barristers at law. The conviction produced on the minds of these gentlemen was that Ellis's case was one of extreme doubt, and so strong was that conviction that they enquired whether some means could not yet be taken to prevent the execution of that man. Mr Keen said he had the power to delay the execution for a few hours, and Mr Gaunt volunteered to go to London on the next train and obtain a final interview with Lord Normanby.

A few lines were then hastily written expressive of the conviction of the subscribers that Ellis, on his own statement, and that of the other two prisoners was innocent; and the paper was signed by Mr Twemlow, Mr Keen, Mr Gaunt, and Mr Lee – who was counsel against the prisoners on both trials. Mr Brutton, and the Rev R. Buckerage, and Mr Gaunt started with it by train at half past one o'clock yesterday. It is extremely doubtful whether this application will be of any avail. The other two men will certainly be executed. The execution will be delayed until Mr Gaunt's return, which is expected by the train arriving at Stafford at one o'clock this afternoon (Saturday) and will therefore take place between one and two o'clock.

In expectation of the execution taking place on Saturday last, a great number of persons arrived at Stafford on the Friday night and the Saturday morning. The railway trains we are told brought some hundreds, and gigs and spring carts loaded with the admirers of the tragical, were exceedingly numerous. The pedestrians were not a few. It is expected that a large concourse of persons will be present on the awful occasion today.

Of the wretched men themselves we regret to state that we can give no very favourable account. Owen has been kept apart from the other two. Thomas and Ellis have not been separated. Owen positively denies having ill treated the deceased woman in any way whatever. He stated that she submitted without any objection to his embraces twice, at a comparatively early period of the voyage, and that he had nothing to do with her destruction; that Thomas was steering when she was lost. He intimates that Thomas had connection with her against her will. He does not appear to implicate Ellis. Thomas all along – until yesterday, most pertinaciously denied his guilt, and invariably stated that Owen was steering when the woman was lost. Even so late as yesterday morning, Owen having been brought again into the cell where he and Ellis were, a most unseemly and angry contention between them, each charging the other with knowing the last of the woman. They seemed to entertain the most malignant feelings toward each other, and the governor was obliged again to separate them. Later in the day however, when the chaplain had pointed out the awful consequences of telling falsehoods on the verge of the eternal world, Thomas relieved his mind so far as to admit 'that he might have been steering at the time that the woman was lost; and that he might have pushed her into the water; but he was so drunk he did not know what he did.' Thomas yesterday became a completely altered man – he had before exhibited an awful hardihood and recklessness. Yesterday he manifested a broken spirit, and wept bitterly, although he had never before shed a tear. He exonerates Ellis, declaring that he was asleep when it happened. Ellis has always appeared to possess more feeling than the other two, and has uniformly asserted his innocence. He acknowledges however having attempted to violate the woman, though he states he did not effect his object.

The Rev R. Buckeridge, the chaplain, spent the whole of yesterday with these unhappy men, and had previously used his best efforts to bring them to a proper state of mind.

Every preparation was being made yesterday by the governor of the prison for the execution. The drop will be erected this morning at an early hour, but the execution itself is not expected to take place as we have already stated until one or two o'clock.

SATURDAY MORNING – WE STOP THE PRESS TO ANNOUNCE!

That a Queen's messenger has arrived at the county gaol with further respite for William Ellis. It is expected that the execution of Owen and Thomas will take place at One o'clock this afternoon.

SECOND EDITION

THE EXECUTION OF JAMES OWEN AND GEORGE THOMAS alias DOBELL FOR MURDER

These wretched men have this day expiated their dreadful crime by the forfeiture of their lives upon the gallows. Vast numbers of persons from all parts of the country, the majority of who were from the lowest class of life, including a large number of females, crowded into Stafford at an early hour in the morning, indeed many arrived the previous night, and the beds at most of the public houses in the town were engaged for the occasion.

We have already mentioned that Thomas became greatly softened yesterday, and made a very important admission. He and likewise Ellis confessed that their general habits had been of the most depraved and profligate character; though not differing much from the class of men to which they belonged. We understand that it was most painful to hear their account of the scenes which are of daily occurrence amongst boatmen. Thieving it is reckoned is an accomplishment, and those men are most sought after by captains of boats, who can pilfer the cargoes most adroitly and to the greatest extent. They say there is no difficulty in disposing of the stolen goods, receivers being on hand at all points of the canals. It is an invariable practice to abstract ale, spirits etc from the casks, by means of siphon pumps which are in common use on the boats. Drunkenness is consequently habitual amongst boatmen to a dreadful extent, and as intemperance is the fruitful parent of crime, they are generally found prepared for the perpetration of the worst description of offences. Fornication and adultery are commonly prevalent. As to religion, they pay no regard whatever to even its forms. Thomas and Ellis having acknowledged that they don't remember having ever been in a church or any other place of worship. They made statements to this effect, and to a greater extent to the Reverend Chaplain respecting their own criminal courses, and those of their fellow boatmen generally.

This morning at an early hour, the Reverend Chaplain visited the men in their cells, giving them advice suitable to their awful situation, and offering up fervent prayers in their presence, and on their behalf. The reverend gentleman was assisted in his solemn duties by the Reverend Edward Rathbone; the governor likewise occasionally giving them a word of advice. Thomas was much more firm than he was yesterday, and denied any knowledge of what happened to the woman after the boat had gone a little way beyond Colwich lock. He repeated what he had said before, that he was 'very drunk' and was unconscious of the manner by which she came to her end. If he was steering at the time, it was unknown to him. He most solemnly confirmed that he had nothing more to confess. Ellis likewise persisted in his former statements, and denied most positively any knowledge of the manner in which the woman was drowned. Owen also declared he had no further disclosure to make, having told the whole truth on the subject of the death of the woman.

Although a respite had been received on behalf of Ellis during the course of the night, the deputy sheriff considered it best not to disturb the arrangement respecting the time of the execution, which had been fixed for one o'clock, after the arrival of the first London train.

The drop was erected at an early hour in the morning in front of the county prison, and two halters were suspended from the cross beam. Barricades were placed at the three approaches to the drop to keep the crowd off. Great numbers of persons began to collect by ten or eleven o'clock and the multitude became more dense as the hour of execution approached. About 12 o'clock, the three culprits were summoned from their cells to the chapel of the prison in order to partake of the sacrament. The scene on their entrance was most solemn. Owen and Thomas knelt on one side of the communion table, the governor of the prison and Ellis on the other; the Reverend and his associate kneeling at the two ends. Before the solemn service commenced, the chaplain addressed these wretched men with great solemnity, entreating them as in the presence of Almighty God, and as those who would in a brief space be uttered into the eternal world, to confess the whole truth and not to go into the presence of their maker with a lie in their mouth. In reply to this solemn appeal, Owen said – 'I have nothing more to say' – Thomas said 'I have told all' – Ellis made no remark.

The conduct of the men was very becoming and devout. The firmness of Owen and Thomas was truly remarkable. Ellis alone appearing a great deal depressed in spirits. Owen and Thomas were supplied with prayer books, which they held with an unwavering hand, and repeated the responses with an audible voice, particularly Owen whose utterance was very distinct and apparently devotional. Ellis not being able to read had no book. The chaplain went through the service in a manner the most impressive and affecting, though his utterance occasionally was almost overpowered by the strength of his emotions. The few who witnessed this solemn scene will never forget it. At its conclusion, Owen and Thomas were conducted to the press room. Ellis remained and was then informed by the governor for the first time that Her Majesty had been pleased to respite his execution. The governor communicated this information in a most feeling manner, and Ellis received it in a very proper spirit: he wept much and appeared thankful for the mercy extended to him.

The Reverend Chaplain then addressed him in a most affecting and impressive strain, imploring him to give God thanks for his deliverance from immediate death, and to spend his prolonged life in prayer and praise. Ellis received the admonition with every expression of gratitude and determination to attend to the advice he had received. At his own request he was then conducted to the press room, to take leave of Owen and Thomas. The governor accompanied him and made known to the other two that a further respite had been received for Ellis, and that he would not be executed with them. On this communication being made, it was difficult to ascertain which of the men felt the most acutely. Ellis burst into tears, and taking each of his former associates by the hand, kissed them most affectionately, and exclaimed repeated – 'God bless you dear boys.'

This conduct of Ellis appeared to overcome the feelings of both men, particularly of Owen, who wept bitterly. Thomas addressing Ellis said 'Bill, if you get off, let this be a warning to you as long as you live.' When he left the room, he continued to exclaim 'God bless you.' The governor, Chaplain and few attendants who were present, in vain endeavoured to restrain their feelings. The scene was indescribably affecting. When Owen and Thomas met, we were glad to perceive that they had become perfectly reconciled to each other. They shook hands very cordially. The executioner then proceeded to pinion the arms of Owen and Thomas, and while that was proceeding, R. W. Hand Esq. the deputy Sheriff arrived, announcing that Mr Gaunt from London, with a communication from Lord Normanby conforming the respite of Ellis. His Lordship had expressed his satisfaction to Mr Gaunt that he had received the certificate on behalf of Ellis, since it corresponded with his own view of the case. With regard to the other two, the law must take its course.

The period of execution was now publicly announced by the solemn sound of the prison bell.

'The dying knell told for the living men.'

Soon afterwards the mournful procession moved from the press room to the lodge of the county prison. The Chaplain walked first, reading the funeral service of the Church of England, followed by the two culprits and the executioner and governor and officers of the prison. The men walked with a firm step and ascended the steps of the drop without assistance. The executioner immediately placed the ropes round their necks, shook hands with them, and as the Chaplain pronounced the words 'In the midst of life we are in death' the fatal bolt was drawn, and the wretched men ceased to live. Being both robust men, their bodies were much convulsed. They appeared to be in the act of prayer up to the moment they were turned off, and made no remark on the drop. After hanging an hour, their bodies were cut down, and would be interred within the precincts of the prison.

The concourse of persons who witnessed the execution was unprecedentedly great. It is supposed that there were nearly ten thousand persons present. Every spot, remote and near from which a view of the drop could be obtained was occupied. Walls, trees, roofs of houses etc being fixed upon by many as convenient places from where to view the scene. The three thoroughfares approaching the gaol were densely crowded as far as the sight could reach, and the neighbouring gardens were filled with people. No peculiar feeling was displayed when the men made their appearance on the drop, though when it fell, the females who were very numerous, gave partial vent to their emotions.

In consequence of the vast influx of persons, several influential individuals applied to the borough magistrates to have a body of special constables sworn in. Accordingly T. Stephenson Esq Mayor, and J. Roger Esq. Justice, appointed a number of special constables to act in case of need. Happily their services were not required. The crowd behaved with decorum, and began quietly to disperse soon after the conclusion of the tragic scene.

We cannot close our account of this melancholy event without expressing our thanks to the governor and Chaplain of the county prison, for the courtesy with which they have on our application supplied us with any information respecting these unfortunate men, which they thought it was proper to communicate to the public.

Ellis's life will be spared.

IN CONCLUSION

Did the whole truth and nothing but the truth come out in court? Far from it. Certainly, if a similar case happened today, the forensic experts would be amongst the first on the scene and would thereafter sift carefully through the body and clothes of the deceased to find definitive DNA evidence of any rape. But this kind of knowledge was lacking in 1840, and the evidence of the surgeon was far from helpful, though it is interesting that the internal organs were examined – a start of CSI.

And then there is the testimony of Joseph Orgill, the bigamist. And honest though he may very well have been, it is very doubtful in modern times whether his relating of a conversation of a cell mate would be enough to bring about a retrial. So, in essence, we the readers of this account are pretty much in the same position as the jury back in 1840. Our minds are full of suspicion, as we mentally imagine the journey of the Pickford boat and its occupants as they make their way from Stoke on Trent to Fradley. Did Owen and Thomas rape Christina Collins? Probably. Did they bring about her death? Probably; but the evidence to put a rope around their necks is admittedly flimsy and circumstantial. Also, one thinks of the boy, Musson – surely he knew more than he let on in court, as we see from one account that he was driving the boat between Colwich Lock and Brindley's Bank; but if so, he no doubt took that knowledge with him to his own grave many years later.

As I mentioned in the introduction to this book, the story of Christina Collins has been told in short versions elsewhere; but at this juncture, perhaps we could wonder what sort of person she was? Certainly, from the former narrative, it appears that she was a slightly built, modest sort of a person, with fine moral habits. One publication gave a little more background to this enigmatic lady, though I must add that I cannot confirm the account, not having discovered the original documents, but here it is:

When young, Christina married initially, to a much older man, a certain Thomas Ingleby, who worked as a Magician and was renowned as The Emperor of all

Conjurers. Thomas toured the land delivering his performances, parts of which were not for the squeamish. One of his popular tricks was to slaughter a live chicken on stage, pass the bloody head around and then apparently resurrect the dead chicken – obviously it was a second chicken that must have been a remarkable clone from the first. The account tells us that Christina travelled with her husband and went on to assist him on the stage by dancing, singing, and assisting in some of the tricks. It was only when this much older man died, that she remarried and this time to the Robert Collins that we met in court.

NOTE ON HANGINGS

In Britain, death by hanging was the principal form of execution from Anglo-Saxon times until capital punishment was abolished in 1964. Up to 1868, all hangings were carried out in public and attracted large crowds, who were at least supposed to be deterred by the spectacle, but who more probably went for the morbid excitement and the carnival atmosphere that usually surrounded such events. And when one asks the question whether severe penalties deter a criminal from his acts, it is of note that pickpockets were not deterred from committing their crimes by seeing other pickpockets hanging for the very same offence. The modern expression Gala Day is derived from the Anglo-Saxon gallows day. After hangings retreated inside prisons, large crowds would still often gather outside the gates to see the posting of the death notice, or to protest the execution.

EXECUTION STATISTICS

At the beginning of the nineteenth century, there were no fewer than 222 capital crimes, including such terrible offences as impersonating a Chelsea pensioner and damaging London Bridge! One reason why the number of capital crimes was so high was due to the way that particular offences were broken down into specific crimes. For instance, stealing in a shop, a dwelling house, a warehouse and a brothel were each separate offences. Similarly with arson: burning down a house was distinguished from burning a hayrick. It should be noted that in practice, there were only about seventeen general offences for which a death sentence was carried out in the eighteenth and early nineteenth centuries. These included murder, attempted murder, arson, rape, sodomy, forgery, uttering (passing forged or counterfeit monies or bills), coining, robbery, highway robbery (in many cases, this was the offence of street robbery, that we would now call mugging), housebreaking, robbery in a dwelling house, returning from transportation, cutting and maiming (grievous bodily harm), and horse, cattle or sheep stealing. For all the other capital offences, transportation to America or Australia was generally substituted for execution.

In the period from 1735 to 1964, there were some 10,935 civilian executions in England and Wales alone, comprising 10,378 men and 557 women. The last hangings of all in Britain, were two carried out simultaneously at 8 a.m. on 13 August 1964 at Walton prison, Liverpool, and Strangeways prison in Manchester, when Peter Anthony Allen and Gwynne Owen Evans were executed for the murder of John West. Ruth Ellis was the last woman to suffer the death penalty in Britain on 13 July 1955.

Up to 1877, the short drop was generally utilised, after which the long drop from 5-8 feet was used as a more humane practice. With the long drop, the prisoner fell quickly and was brought to a quick stop by the rope, which usually snapped the vertebrae and spinal cord, causing a speedy death. With the former method, a person could hang for two to three minutes in agony as they were slowly strangled. On occasions, the struggle was followed by a lull, after which the body was thrown into convulsions as the legs were drawn up to the chest (hence the expression in the former trial – much convulsed). This stage is thought to take place after the prisoner has lost consciousness. A hood was used as much for the benefit of onlookers, as watching a person's eyes bulge, their tongue stick out and the face go blue was a most shocking sight. Countries such as Iran still use hanging as a method of execution, and there will always be a debate about whether the death penalty should be brought back for serious offences such as murder. Some may argue that perhaps lethal injection is a more humane and quick way to despatch a criminal; but when one looks at the records in the US, it is patently clear that many of those executions were botched in a variety of ways, and indeed caused severe suffering before the person was announced dead.

There are several recorded instances of revival in this country during the seventeenth and eighteenth centuries. One of the most famous is that of John Smith, hanged at Tyburn on Christmas Eve 1705. Having been turned off the back of the cart, he dangled for fifteen minutes until the crowd began to shout 'reprieve', whereupon he was cut down and taken to a nearby house, where he soon recovered. He was asked what it had felt like to be hanged and this is what he told his rescuers:

When I was turned off, I was for some time sensible of very great pain occasioned by the weight of my body and felt my spirits in strange commotion, violently pressing upwards. Having forced their way to my head I saw a great blaze or glaring light that seemed to go out of my eyes in a flash and then I lost all sense of pain. After I was cut down, I began to come to myself and the blood and spirits forcing themselves into their former channels put me by a prickling or shooting into such intolerable pain that I could have wished those hanged who had cut me down.

HANGING OF NAZIS AFTER THE SECOND WORLD WAR

Experiments were carried out by F. E. Buckland, the assistant director of pathology, British Army of the Rhine, on Nazi war criminals executed by the British at Hameln Prison in Germany after the Second World War, and these found, that although the prisoners were rendered unconscious by the drop, the heart could continue to beat for up to twenty-five minutes after execution. This created a problem because it meant that it would take far longer to carry out the batches of executions. It was thus proposed that the medical officer present would inject 10 cc of chloroform into the prisoner 30 seconds after the drop had been given. It was found that if the chloroform was injected directly into the heart it immediately stopped beating, and if injected intravenously into the arm, the heart would stop in seconds. This procedure was first used at the execution of ten men and three women on 13 December 1945.

CHAPTER 9

The Murder of Jane Doley at Wolverhampton Top Lock, 1875

Wolverhampton Top Lock is the location for our final murder. A view of the scene today is very different from what life was like here at the start of the twentieth century. In the photograph taken from roughly that period, we see a flurry of boating activity, as craft and their hard-worked crews arrive either from the upward journey through the twenty-one locks from Aldersley or from the BCN to go down the same. Men and horses can be seen taking a brief respite as they wait their turn to go through the lock. The canal basin that features much in this story is the one going off to the left. In the past, this was quite a long arm with room for several full-length narrow boats to moor up; today it has been left as only a short stub. This was the very busy Victoria Basin, which was an important loading and unloading point for Wolverhampton town. Top Lock is only a stone's throw from the bustling town centre, but as with all waterways, the canal, even though surrounded by the continual flow of motor vehicles navigating the modern ring road, remains aloof and independent.

Located some yards from Top Lock and the canal houses is the old former warehouse of Fellows, Morton & Clayton, and at the time of our crime, the company provided stabling for the many boat horses that hauled the unpowered narrow boats around the system. Michael Pearson in his guide to the BCN relates that men known as 'hobblers' used to congregate around Top Lock to offer their services to any boat captains who needed an extra hand negotiating the long line of locks – for a small fee of course. But now to get down to our murder.

The dreadful incident happened on Monday 22 December 1902, but the mystery of who perpetrated this heinous crime was to plague the Wolverhampton police force for the best part of the next ten years. That the dead woman was the victim of a brutal, vicious attack was never in question, but despite several arrests, prime suspects and numerous police court hearings, the Wolverhampton law men of one hundred years ago were never fully able to unravel the sordid details of the case.

It is not surprising really that the detectives had a hard time finding any really concrete evidence to point to their elusive prey, for the whole affair was entangled in the grim underworld that the canal, its rootless society, and the slum-ridden periphery provided. Boatmen and their families were there one day and gone the next, and certainly even the canal companies only had a vague idea of where they might be. Added to that, the area was surrounded by beer houses, rough lodging houses, and unemployment that caused vulnerable and

Wolverhampton Top Lock in the early twentieth century, when there was considerable boating activity at this point. Victoria Basin is top left.

poor women to sell their bodies for whatever they could get to pay for the next meal.

Wolverhampton was much like the other large cities of the day, and its poor quarter was filled with back-to-back housing that was often crammed to capacity with several beds or the more common straw-filled sacks. The lodging houses provided a roof and very basic amenities for a transient population that included boatmen and others who worked on the Great Western Railway. Spit and sawdust pubs could be found on every corner, vying for the clamouring trade of boatmen and other labourers. And as we have seen from our earlier accounts in London, drinking was one of the main pursuits of the working man. Rowdy language, street brawls, illegal gambling, and all the other manifestations of petty crime abounded. Having said that, murders were rare, and when they did occur, it appeared that the whole community seemed to be in shock.

Jane Doley, a married woman in her mid-forties, was a familiar face in the alehouses on that side of Wolverhampton near Victoria Basin. Mr Doley, her husband, lived in Wood Street, with a son who had recently left school, and another who was said to be away soldiering. But Jane had lived apart from her family for eighteen months, and had resided since Christmas 1901 at a lodging house in Stafford Street. Her night-time trade put her at the mercies of the roughest types.

Around 6 a.m., on the cold morning of 22 December, local labourer Edgar Jenkins was walking along Southampton Street, which lies parallel to the basin, and Littles

Lane (Littles Lane Bridge is below Top Lock) and close to the premises of the Great Western Railway company. As he approached the Victoria Basin, he stumbled upon what he at first thought was a pile of sacks, as it was still quite dark. On striking a match, he discovered to his horror under its flickering pool of light, the sprawled body of a woman. She had been dead for some time, but her face was frozen into an expression of terror, while her features were cut and bruised, and her hair was matted with blood.

Obviously shocked and repulsed by his findings, Jenkins ran quickly away to the nearest police station in Springfield. Police Constable Morgan was soon at Victoria basin along with his superior, Inspector Henry Purchase, and his boss, the head of Wolverhampton Police, Captain Burnett. And despite the early discovery of the body, the news of the ghastly event speedily swept through the local alleys, so that an excited and interested crowd had gathered to witness the grisly scene. The police then endeavoured to keep the nosiest onlookers from disturbing the crime scene; but even to their hardened gaze, this was a sick sight. The poorly dressed corpse lay in a crumpled heap on a slight mound, adjacent to a corrugated outbuilding, which was spattered with her blood. Jane's black straw hat lay on the ground nearby, close to a torn silk handkerchief, which was thought to belong to a boatman.

The coroner's mortuary cart arrived much later at 9 a.m., too late to spare the workers of Danks & Walker the ordeal of having to go to work within yards of the feet of the poor deceased. On the following day, a Coroner's Inquest was convened in front of R. A. Wilcock, and the brief facts of the case were presented to the court. Jane Doley had been positively identified by an estranged but shocked

Wolverhampton Top Lock in more recent years, when the Victoria Basin had long gone.

husband, and the sorry depths to which her life had sunk were related to the assembled listeners.

Her life had held few prospects, and her death had left even fewer possessions. Fellow lodgers told how she was 'hard up' and often went without a morsel to eat. Items that were discovered in her skirt pocket included two pawn tickets dating back to October. Apparently, she was well known about the town, often to be seen sitting on one of the seats in the open space in front of the old church, in company with her widowed sister. With no immediate suspects, Mr Wilcock adjourned the hearing for two weeks, during which time Jane Doley received a pauper's funeral.

And, while Christmas of 1902 carried on in much the same way as usual for Wolverhampton folk and its boatmen and women, Captain Burnett and his constables were hard at work trying to uncover any clues that might lead them to the perpetrator of the crime committed on their patch. Just over a week later, there appeared to be a major breakthrough in the case. This was timely, as there was much pressure on the police to apprehend the killer and put the locals' minds at ease that a further atrocity would not follow. The bobbies entered the cold and usually grim underworld of lodging houses, charged with the painstaking task of questioning all they met. A certain Thomas Nash, a shoemaker residing at Hinde's lodging house in Pipers Row, reported to the police that on 27 December, he heard fellow lodger Martin Brown muttering to himself that he had killed a woman, and didn't know what to do.

Brown was employed as a labourer emptying the many coal boats that visited the wharf. He was promptly arrested as the chief suspect. Investigations that followed demonstrated that he had often been seen in the company of the deceased, and had been in the habit of drinking with her at the Four Ashes Inn as soon as he had received his wages on Saturday afternoons. When placed in the dock, Brown vehemently denied that he had even seen Jane Doley on the day that she had been killed. For a change, he had been visiting the Barley Mow in Pipers Row; and as for the charge by Nash that he had somehow confessed to the crime – well, that was completely untrue, and if he had mentioned it, it had been just some drunken rambling. Other witnesses from the local lodging houses were called to give evidence, but this was so erratic and held in such low esteem by the court, that it was found impossible to reach any conclusions.

When questioned why Nash would have made such allegations if it were not true, Brown undermined Nash's testimony by claiming that Nash was a rough sort who was capable of saying anything. With Nash discredited, the coroner then dismissed the case against Brown as unreliable. The inquiry thus ended with an open verdict. The police knew that someone out there had the information that they required, but were unable to break the ring of silence. A solid conviction seemed as elusive as ever. The months rolled by, boatmen and their families went up and down the twenty-one Wolverhampton locks, and it appeared to many that this case would never be solved. And then, seemingly out of the blue, almost two years later, a former soldier who had just returned to the area restarted the investigation. Thomas Green, of No. 9 court, Littles Lane, had at the time of the murder been a soldier serving with the Royal North Lancashire Regiment of Foot, on leave in the town. Since leaving the army, he had started work as a boatman.

Two years previously, whilst living in Old Mill Street, just off the Five Ways, Green had been in the habit of meeting Jane Doley, and he admitted to having known her for five years. He claimed that on the evening prior to the discovery of her body, they had drunk together in the Little Swan until 10 p.m. The pair then returned to his

Boat passing through Wolverhampton Top Lock.

house nearby. Much later, around 1.45 a.m., hours before she was murdered, Brown had escorted her back to Five Ways, where standing underneath a lamp was a man he recognised. This man whistled to Jane, and she went away with him. That was the last that Thomas Green saw of her. It was only later in the day that he learned of her untimely demise.

It appears that Green then went on to relate this tale to several of his drinking pals, and it wasn't long before someone turned him in to the police. They then took him along to the station to make a full statement. The man who Green implicated as being the last person to see Jane Doley alive was one Peter Kelly, who was promptly arrested on St Valentine's day 1905 outside the Union Inn, Canal Street, a much-used pub by the local boatmen. This caused a flurry of local speculation that at last the killer had been apprehended, and quite a crowd followed the arrested man to the station. Kelly was described as a typical boatman, rough looking, with the usual loose scarf, and wearing pearl buttons on his jacket. He was subsequently charged with the wilful murder of the woman before Wolverhampton Magistrates on Thursday 16 February that same year. But the case was by no means successfully concluded.

For a second time, the judicial process was thwarted by unreliable and insufficient evidence. And to add to the confusion, Thomas Green, the chief witness, was himself arrested on the following day for having assaulted another witness, Edith Holloway. It seems that Green had seen Holloway visit the detective's office in Red Lion Street on the day of the hearing and jumped to the conclusion that she had been pointing the finger of accusation at him. After an argument, he struck her out in the street, and it transpires that there had been bad blood between the two. Green was then fined

10s for his assault upon that witness. When he said that he could not pay the fine, he was duly locked up.

Meanwhile, Kelly firmly denied having anything to do with Jane Doley's death, and with no other evidence against him than Green's, he was set free. From that date on, the investigation wound down and the killer of poor Jane Doley was never found, forever hidden in an underworld of slums, petty crime and poverty. And so, if you happen to be cranking paddles up and down, either on your way up or down that well-worn flight, you may pause for a brief moment to consider how very different life was at this place over one hundred years ago.

CHAPTER 10

Troubled Waters: A Nineteenth-Century Feud between the BCN and Edward Elwell

In the last quarter of the eighteenth and the first half of the nineteenth century, water was needed not only for domestic and industrial purposes as it is today, but also for transport and energy. Before the steam engine had become both efficient and economic – and indeed for long afterwards – water was a staple means of inland communication and a relatively cheap source of power. The canals and the mills were dependant on it, and as the industrial revolution advanced, and the canals and mills grew in number, so the pressures on supplies of water, which remained static, increased. This led to rivalry and much litigation between competing canal companies and between canal companies and mill owners. An epic example of this was the long drawn-out dispute between the Birmingham Canal Navigations Company (BCN) and the owners of the Wednesbury Forge.

The BCN had a bad reputation. It was said to be high-handed, ruthless and unscrupulous. There was from its beginning a conflict between those of its promoters who thought it should be primarily a public service, and those for whom profit was paramount. One of its promoters, the Birmingham industrialist Samuel Garbett, an ancestor of the Archbishop of York, alleged that the company's proceedings had been arbitrary and offensive, and had shown tendencies to establish a dangerous monopoly.

According to Charles Hadfield (*The Canals of the West Midlands*), 'From the time of the opening of the first section, the company was accused of high-handedness and monopoly, of illegal seizure of land, illegal entry into other people's property, etc.' Whether these accusations were well-founded or merely the product of commercial rivalry, it may now be impossible to establish. There was, however, one episode in the early history of the company that suggests that the directors were on occasions less than scrupulous.

On 13 December 1771, a Mr Bache waited on the board of directors to demonstrate the model of a machine he had invented for 'the breaking of the ice in severe weather.' The director's immediate reaction was favourable. They thought the machine ingenious, and likely to answer the intended purpose. Mr James Brindley, the company's celebrated consulting engineer, who was present at the demonstration, agreed, and it was arranged that he should meet Mr Bache the next morning to see if any alteration or improvement can be struck out (*sic*) to render the model more extensively useful, and that Mr Bache be requested to attend the committee on Friday night next, against which time they will more fully consider the subject and then be glad to confer with Mr Bache upon the scheme being carried into execution.

The company's minute book does not reveal what the outcome of Brindley's meeting with Bache was, or whether the committee subsequently conferred with the inventor. What they do seem to have done was to have appropriated his invention, for the following month, the company's resident engineer, Samuel Bull, signified to the committee that he had thought of a machine for – breaking the ice – which might be made at the expense of four or five pounds. As for poor Mr Bache, one of the directors was to tell him that the committee would 'consider further of the machine proposed to them, and will pay a proper regard to the trouble he has been upon the occasion'. Nearly three years elapsed before the committee carried out their intention to pay a 'proper regard'. On 9 December 1774, they resolved that five guineas should be paid as a 'compliment' to Mr Bache for his trouble.

Twenty years later, there was another collision between another individual and the company. An extension of the canal had been planned to run from Broadwaters (Bilston) to Walsall. The landowners along the proposed line of the canal had all, with a few exceptions, given their assent. The main exception was Edward Elwell, who owned about two and a half acres near the junction of Pleck Lane and the Wednesbury-Darlaston road, on the site of the future Victoria Ironworks. The land was occupied by James Atkins, who also opposed the company's plan, as did the tenant of the adjacent property. This was John Woodward, whose memory is now preserved in two Walsall streets – Woodward's Road and Woodward's Place. He was quite probably related to, if not the father of, another Woodward who figures later in our story. As for Edward Elwell, he and his brother William, twice Mayor of Walsall, were iron founders, whose works at Great Bridge were also alongside the canal.

Edward's opposition failed, and the new branch was dug as planned, bisecting his property. Some of the resulting ill will may well have rubbed off on his nephew, another Edward, then aged twelve, and may have been a factor in the latter's long feud with the BCN.

It all began in July 1838. Edward had been the proprietor of Wednesbury Forge since 1817, and there he manufactured edge tools almost exclusively intended for export. The machinery at the works was driven by both steam and water power. The water that turned the five great mill wheels came from the River Tame, which flowed past the works. At least forty other mills were dependant on the Tame and its minor tributaries, and so, to some extent, was the BCN. Ultimately, the BCN as a whole came into contact with the Tame and its main feeders at a variety of locations, which should have flowed either into it, over weirs in the canal or through culverts under it. And at this point I will go into a small aside regarding the River Tame.

The main source of the Tame starts as a small stream in between Oldbury and West Bromwich on the northern side of the Rowley Hills, and winds north-east toward Great Bridge. From Great Bridge, it describes a circle towards Wednesbury before heading toward Pleck (where our trouble occurs) and on to Hampstead. Although the Tame only receives three small tributaries from the West Bromwich area within the first bend, it is better served by the acquisition of a number of left-bank streams that included the Tipton Brook, the Leabrook, the Willenhall brook, the Walsall Tame (the one that feeds Elwell's works), and runs through Caldmore and the Fullbrook. For such a small stream, the upper part of a river system, the Tame has little fall, and from the 450 contour to the 400-foot contour, it has covered a distance of two and a half miles, a gradient of 1:264, while there is an even gentler fall of only fifty feet over the next four and a half miles. And it was these comparatively small waterways which were providing so much power to the mills in the eighteenth and nineteenth centuries.

In order to keep the locks and the highest levels of the canal supplied with water, four steam pumps were installed at Ocker Hill, the first in 1784, the second in 1791, the third in 1802, and the fourth in 1826. It was the constant operation of these pumps which were the immediate cause of Edward Elwell's complaint against the company. He maintained that, but for them, water would have overflowed from the canal into the Tame, and thence to Wednesbury Forge. Because it did not, the forge suffered a corresponding loss of power for which compensation should be paid by the company.

The first shot in Elwell's campaign was fired on 23 July 1838, when he gave notice of damage and a claim for compensation. The notice was ignored, as was a second given in January 1839. A third notice in April was backed by a claim for £4,000 for damages already sustained, and for £10,000 for damages likely to be sustained in the future. This fell on equally deaf ears, and in January 1840, Elwell issued a writ against the company summoning them to empanel a jury to assess the damages he was suffering. Provision for such a procedure had been made under the Acts of Parliament by which the company was regulated. After a delay of several months, a jury was empanelled and appears to have found in Elwell's favour, but subject to questions of law, which were later referred to the court of Queen's Bench.

In the meantime, Elwell suggested, via his solicitor, Francis Woodward of Wednesbury, that the company should buy the forge. This suggestion was not as surprising as it sounds, for the company had been known to buy mills with whose owners they were in dispute. However, they were not interested in Elwell's offer, and further propositions made by him in 1843 were dismissed as 'wholly inadmissible'.

Litigation being resumed, the company were informed in March 1845 that their solicitor had received briefs for argument in the court of Queen's Bench, which the company hoped the Solicitor General, having lately returned from abroad, would be able to attend. Judgment was given in the company's favour in the following January. This was by no means the end of the affair, and from 1846 to 1849, it was being considered by an arbitrator or referee. Mr Sergeant Clarke's subsequent 'determination' was not at all to the company's liking. Clarke was a local man, and recorder of Walsall, and the company may have suspected him of bias.

Old Bailey court
scene.

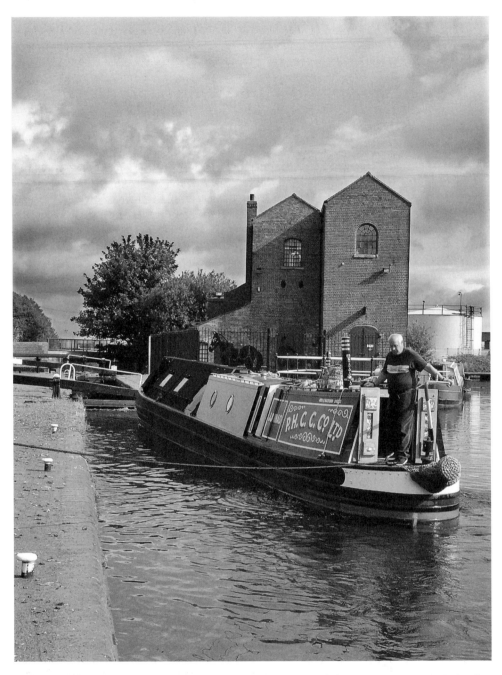

Titford, Oldbury; one of the last remaining pumping stations left on the BCN. Now utilised for meetings of the local canal society.

They contemplated applying again to the court of Queen's Bench, but their counsel, Phipson, recommended in December 1848 they should not, as their application could not succeed. All of this suggests that Elwell's grounds for complaint were not ill-founded. However, despite Phipson's advice, application was made to the court of Queen's Bench, which again found in the BCN's favour.

Convinced as he was of the justice of his cause, Elwell appealed to the next higher court, that of Exchequer of Chamber. The case was expected to be argued in November 1849, but it was not heard until the following February, when judgment was yet again given in favour of the defendants. Elwell then appealed to the highest court in the land, the House of Lords. The appeal was heard in June 1852, and on 26 June, judgment was once more given in favour of the BCN. Costs amounting to £459 14s 11d were awarded to the company. This was in addition to the £3,000 costs already awarded by the two lower courts. In January 1853, the company's solicitor reported that Elwell's solicitor had paid £1,200 in satisfaction of the company's claim for costs, charges and expenses (sic) of the late law suits with him. He had spent on them, at a conservative estimate, the equivalent of almost £250,000.

Despite what would have seemed the *coup de grâce*, and despite the expenses, Elwell had evidently not yet given up hope of obtaining compensation from the company. Their solicitor reported also in January 1853 that Mr Elwell had called on him and intimated his intention of making further claims against the company in reference to his allegation that this company had abstracted water from the brooks and streams supplying Mr Elwell's forge, and should take proceedings at law unless the company provide him with some supply of water in dry seasons. However, it appears that Elwell does not seem to have carried out this threat.

It was not long in any case before a further opportunity arose for him to harry the company. In 1855, a Bill was presented to Parliament to empower the BCN to make a canal and tunnel from the Birmingham level near Dudley Port to 'That part of the Birmingham canal called the Netherton canal, near the Windmill End furnaces.'

Petitions were entered against the Bill by Lord Ward (which is in itself odd, because when the tunnel was commenced, Lord Ward cut the first sod), the Oxford, Worcester & Wolverhampton Railway, and Messrs Edward Elwell – Senior and Junior. This was reported to the directors of the canal on 23 February 1855 by their solicitor, who also told them that Messrs Elwell have by their solicitor written to the company's Parliamentary Agents to enquire whether the promoters were disposed to make any proposals which may obviate the incurring of expenses of opposing the Bill in Committee, and that the solicitor had answered the Application stating that the company's clerk would see Mr Elwell Junior.

If such a meeting took place, it was abortive, for the Elwells' objections to the Bill were pressed vigorously by their counsel before the select committee, which considered them on 22, 23 and 26 March, and 17 and 18 April. The first witness to be examined was Robert Thomas, the company's secretary since 1843. The Elwells' counsel, Johnson, sought to demonstrate that the new canal would need more water, and this would have to be pumped up from the lower or Walsall level, with a consequent reduction in the volume that would reach the Tame and thus Wednesbury Forge. Thomas denied that this would be so, but he did admit that the company's reservoirs had been greatly enlarged, and that the power of the pumps had been progressively increased.

When Johnson started to question Thomas on the conduct of Elwell's lawsuit against the company, the chairman of the committee intervened to remind him that the committee could not go into Mr Elwell's 'earlier grievances'. Despite Thomas's contention that the proposed new canal could have no effect on the supply of water to Wednesbury Forge, he was persuaded to agree, when examined by James Loch

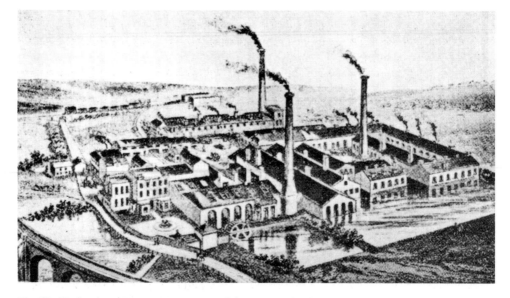

Elwell's Wednesbury Forge. Notice one of the water wheels.

for the defendants, that far from depriving the Elwells of water, the company's operations would be positively advantageous to them.

The next witness to be examined was Philip Williams, the Wednesbury banker and iron master. His evidence on the alleged illegal appropriation by the company of water from the Portway stream, a tributary of the Tame near Oldbury, was thoroughly unsatisfactory. Williams was a most reluctant witness, being both a friend of Edward Elwell and a director of the company. The conflict within him is apparent in exchanges such as

Q. Do you know Mr Elwell?
A. Yes.
Q. In your capacity as a director, has he more than once complained to you?
A. I would rather say nothing about Mr Elwell.
Q. Will you tell me this; do you know of a restriction that prohibits the canal company from diverting or using any of the water of the River Tame or any of its tributaries?
A. It is a dangerous subject; if I do not say what Mr Elwell wishes, we shall not agree. I cannot help him.

When Williams was finally brought to admit that he believed the company were restricted in their use of the water of the Tame and its tributaries, he was again questioned on the Portway stream, and his embarrassment became acute. When asked whether he knew the Portway brook, he replied, 'I do not know any particular brook at Oldbury.' However, a few questions later, it emerged that not only did he know it, but he had actually inspected it at a point where it meets the canal. He told the committee, 'I walked over the ground with Mr Elwell as a friend. I heard all he said but I said nothing in return.'

When pressed to say whether the brook flowed into the canal or bypassed it through a culvert, his answers were devious to the extreme. He could not tell what he saw or where he went. Exasperated, counsel repeated, 'You cannot tell his lordship

[Lord Stanley of Alderley, who had just been appointed president of the Board of Trade] and the members of this committee whether you did then see with your own eyes the water going into the canal.'

'No more than being in this room I could tell where the water went at Westminster Bridge.'

When re-examined by Loch for the company, and asked whether the Bill would affect any rights Mr Elwell had, Williams replied, 'I imagine not.' The note of doubt was, we may hope, attributable more to his desire not to offend a friend than to any weakness he may have suspected in his company's case.

The next witness, William Matthews, JP of Kingswinford, was equally uneasy when being asked questions relating to Elwell. He told counsel, 'I am anxious to avoid coming in contact with Mr Elwell in any way – I cannot do him any good, but I do not wish to do him any disservice.'

The last witness to appear before the committee was as emphatic in his evidence as Williams and Matthews had been vague. He was a Birmingham mining engineer named Brook Ridgway Smith and what he had to say about the company's operations made a powerful impression upon the committee. He told them that the water for the canal was drawn from the Tame and its tributaries, and that the Jim Crow branch of the canal was fed by the Portway stream, which otherwise would have flowed into the Tame, and found its way to Mr Elwell's forge. Smith also showed, with the aid of a model, how the canal was fed with water which flowed into it at the Tividale bridge – presumably Keir's Bridge at Tividale. Smith explained that 'we had to pour the oil through to see where the water went to'. Yet another tributary of the Tame, Spring Vale near Wolverhampton, had, according to the witness, also been diverted to feed the canal.

A model was produced of the Titford weir, and the witness explained how the water was turned into the canal, and found its way via the Jim Crow feeder to the Rotton Park Reservoir. The witness said that the company had done this 'under my own knowledge within the last month' and that it would be a 'detriment to Mr Elwell'. At this point, the company's counsel objected that this evidence related to the existing state of affairs, and not to what might occur should the Bill be passed.

There was then argument between him and Elwell's counsel, upon which the committee room was cleared. After some time, the report of the proceedings recorded – 'the counsel and the parties were again called in.' The chairman stated that the committee had come to the following resolution: that the committee are of the unanimous opinion that they cannot admit evidence on the question of the legality or illegality of the means adopted by the Birmingham Canal Company to supply themselves with water, that question already having been decided by a court of law. The committee feel themselves bound to accept as decisive the judgment of the House of Lords in 1852, founded on the unanimous opinion of the judges to the effect that the canal company are entitled to pump back the water that is brought out of their upper into their lower levels and that such water is not to be considered waste water as long as it can be made available for the purposes of navigation. The committee are of the opinion that the evidence ought to be confined to the question of injury arising to Mr Elwell under the Bill now before them in consequence of the abstraction of water from any sources of supply of which the canal company is not at present possessed.

Elwell's counsel thought he could not show that, and the committee therefore declared that the Preamble of the Bill was proved, or in plain language, the canal company had got what it wanted.

This was the end of Edward Elwell's battle with his over-mighty opponent. He had lost all along the line and had to pay dearly for every stage. One hundred and twenty years later, and taking into account that blood runs thicker than canal water, the

James Watt steam engine.

writer cannot help feeling that, had he based his original suit not on the operation of the Ocker Hill engines, but on the elicit appropriation of the water from the Tame, he might – just might – have won.

A Note about the Boulton & Watt Engines Used on the BCN

The first engines to be installed on the BCN were recirculatory, i.e., they returned water used for lock operations to the top of the locks, and this was always the purpose of the majority of the engines purchased by the BCN. When Brindley had recommended locks instead of a tunnel at Smethwick, he had suggested returning the water by means of 'Fire' engines (as steam engines were then called). But it was not until August 1776 that Mr Henn, the chairman, was asked to have some conversations with Mr Boulton about the erecting of a fire engine in Smethwick. It was to be sited between the (then) seventh and eighth lock (Spon Lane) and was completed and working by April 1778, at a cost of £1,706. It was so successful that a second was ordered and installed at Smethwick, and for some reason it was cheaper then the first. (Discount on steam engines?) And it was the success of these two engines that led the company to purchase the engine that was first fitted at the end of the Ocker Hill arm. The Ocker Hill engine and the arm it was on were higher than the Walsall canal, which was some few hundred yard away, so a tunnel was dug into the hillside to connect the two. The entrance to this tunnel can still be viewed at the end of the Ocker Hill arm, still a popular place for long- and short-term mooring. The Smethwick engine was later taken to the Ocker Hill depot for storage, being used only for demonstrations, and in more recent years, it was transferred to the Birmingham Science Museum and later still to the Birmingham Science Park, where it is now on permanent display, though it could be better illuminated.

Top of James Watt steam engine – Birmingham Science Museum.

And my personal thanks to the Black Country Society for allowing me to reprint this fascinating feud. It was written by C. J. Elwell and appeared first in the *Black Countryman* – the official magazine of the society.

The late C. J. Elwell was a well-respected writer on Black Country topics. He left Oxford without a degree to serve in the Royal Navy during the Second World War. Afterwards he was employed successively by the Foreign Office and Ministry of Defence. His other writings included *Corsican Excursion*, *History of the West Dean Church and Parish*, *St Pauls Wood Green*, *The First Hundred Years*, and he was editor of *A lady of Wednesbury Forge*, also Black Country Society.

Sources for this article were to be found in:

The House of Lords Record Office.
The minute books of the BCN.
S. R. Broadbridge, *The Birmingham Canal Navigations* Vol. 1, 1768-1846 (David and Charles, 1974).
Charles Hadfield, *The Canals of the West Midlands* (David and Charles).
And my own notes from *West Bromwich before the Industrial Revolution*, D. Dilworth.

CHAPTER 11

Moving on to the Twentieth and Twenty-First Centuries

The cases presented in this volume are historical, concentrating on crimes committed in the nineteenth and early twentieth centuries. Nevertheless, most types of crime have continued on with some modern additions. Mugging and drug-dealing are obvious crimes, but others may rightly point out that rudeness is a crime, and complain that some who operate boats on the waterways today show a selfish and arrogant spirit. This has been highlighted by a recent initiative called 'The Considerate Boater' (2008), a philosophy which has been endorsed by organisations large and small. This initiative is not rocket science, but a mixture of real common sense and good working practice, and one wonders why it has not got off the ground before. The advice is free, simple and profound at the same time. The Considerate Boater scheme provides a document and website which says being a considerate boater is simple – think of others in everything you do on the waterways; treat every situation with a smile and a cheery wave; if you have an aggressive nature, then leave it at home. Certainly, this advice is centuries old as exemplified at Matthew 7:12 where Christ said – and I paraphrase – treat others how you would like them to treat you. The Considerate Boater version advocates such things as keeping your music down and not behaving badly after having a drink, before going on to list how to conduct oneself at locks, bridges and when passing other boats, etc. A minority of private boat owners can be rude and thoughtless when they pass hire boaters, thinking – wrongly as it happens – that they are in some way superior to their travelling companions. Indeed, many boat owners started out and learnt their craft by hiring a boat; and let us not forget that it is the hire business that contributes greatly to the upkeep of the canals.

SO WHO'S RESPONSIBLE?

In the past, the waterways were owned/controlled by various private companies and other entities; today, British Waterways now cares for a 2,200-mile network of historic canals and navigable rivers, and they are committed to providing a sustainable future for these precious watery corridors, working to generate the maximum benefits from a unique environment. But to combat crime along canals and rivers they have through necessity partnered themselves with other agencies such as the police force and social boating organisations.

In 2006, BW South East teamed up with Northamptonshire Police and the Environment Agency to launch a leaflet aimed at preventing and encouraging the reporting of crime on the canals and rivers. During the year prior to that initiative, thirty-three crimes were reported on that county's waterways, which included theft, criminal damage and antisocial behaviour. And it appears that these later kinds of crime have increased and thus differentiate between modern times and the earlier years. The leaflet was freely available and distributed to provide useful crime prevention advice and contact numbers for all three agencies. Caroline Hill, enforcement officer for BW, stated that the leaflet urged people to telephone police as their first point of contact when witnessing criminal activity. This sounds simple, but not everyone bothers; it would help if they did.

Certainly many boaters and other visitors to the waterways never experience crime at all, but there do appear to be certain hot spots. Sue Cant, Nene Waterways Operations team leader for EA, said, 'Every year a few boaters and visitors experience crime and antisocial behaviour that inevitably cause upset, inconvenience and unwanted expense.' Yes, it can be quite intimidating to be boating and be attacked by mindless yobs. In 2006, a newspaper headline read – POLICE TO PATROL ROCHDALE CANAL.

> Police officers in North Manchester are joining forces with staff from BW to carry out barge patrols along the Rochdale canal to help reduce crime and antisocial behaviour. The patrols are being set up in Ancoats, Clayton, Miles Platting and Newton Heath in response to growing concerns about robberies, vandalism and nuisance behaviour along the towpath. Over the past six months, BW has recorded eleven incidents of criminal damage, including damage to lock gearing and gates; balance beams were vandalised with machetes, and nearby property was flooded. Regular water and foot patrols in the area will help to reassure people that action is being taken. In October, six barriers were fitted along the towpath to prevent motorcycle riding (this is a common problem and similar measures have been taken throughout the country).

In November 2006, two British Waterway employees involved in the care of West London's canal network were given awards by Chief Supt Ian Thomas from Marine Support Unit for their significant contribution in tackling serious and organised crime (mainly drugs and robbery) on London's waterways. Those awards, normally given to members of the police force, recognised the extraordinary work done in the service of London's inhabitants. London's waterways are again a unique resource contributing greatly to the quality of London as a place to live, work, visit and enjoy, besides acting as a focus for regeneration and development – the upcoming Olympic Games being only one example. Certainly, many initiatives between various bodies have been set up to try and tackle crime within the larger towns and cities:

'Under Lock and Quay' is an advisory document for the London Borough Councils when preparing development briefs and development plan policies for the creation of safe, active and accessible waterside developments. In other words, designers have to take various crimes into consideration when they plan a new building project. The guidance is based upon sound research and reinforces the fact that crime not only impacts upon people and buildings but on a wide variety of built environments. The document continues to say that this is a fine example of how organisations can work in partnership to defeat crime. (Personally I doubt that crime can be defeated, only reduced.)

The document aims to identify the nature of criminal activity, the causes of crime, and the fear of crime – which is not the same thing, as many of us today are somewhat afraid of being a victim – and then provides guidance on the most effective ways of dealing with crime. On initial investigation of police records, it seems that crime along the waterways is relatively minor when compared to that experienced from adjacent areas. However, these same records do not always reflect the full state of waterside-related crime due to the

Truman boat – helping young people to appreciate our wonderful waterways. Wolverhampton Locks.

method by which crimes are reported, while graffiti, threatening behaviour and vandalism often never get into the statistics. Secondly, offences such as burglary of buildings next to the waterway may be recorded by the street address. In 2009, an audacious robbery took place on the Wyrley and Essington, not far from Willenhall, where thieves used a boat to steal and transport away some very expensive metal.

Under Lock and Quay suggests a balanced mix of property uses, including 18/24-hour usage. This diversity enhances the safety of the waterway as a route by generating greater numbers of people next to the waterway, while effective lighting and the presence of CCTV cameras all put off the opportunistic, and perhaps even the professional criminal.

Prevention Better then Cure. When dealing with crime, this has always been the case, and many individuals and groups are wonderfully proactive in getting youngsters onto the waterways. This not only introduces young people to the canals and their history, but it promotes interest and hopefully the sort of respect that prevents them from becoming the kind of vandals that we have already discussed, i.e., those that go along to the canal just to damage the lock beams, etc. Some of those societies include the **National Community Boats Association**, which aims to encourage different groups to use and enjoy our inland waterways. They support social enterprises, caring businesses, youth services, probation and prison services, and school and colleges. The association welcomes all who wish to experience leisure/learning afloat, and is particularly concerned with improving access to boating from disadvantaged communities. Another concern in Walsall, West Midlands, is the **H. F. Truman Narrowboat Committee**. This project began in 1965 with support from the Youth Leaders Council, who built a boat for the young people of the town. The boat *H. F. Truman* was built by Peter Keay (one of the last Midland boat builders) and launched in 1968. They aim to provide narrow boats for young people to be actively involved in educational and recreational pursuits, and to live and work together. **The Surrey Care Trust** operates two boats, one equipped with a wheelchair lift, and provides day trips with well-trained personnel for disadvantaged and disabled people in Surrey. The trust was formed in 1978.

Prisoners at work on the waterways. The use of prisoners to assist in waterway work is not a new initiative but has been used on several historical occasions. During the Second World War, for instance, captured German and Italian troops worked on the BCN and other locations. And certainly there is the well-recorded work in more recent years to restore the Stratford Canal. Recently, a news article stated, 'Prisoners could soon be helping to bridge the skills gap in repair work on a canal. Discussions are underway for inmates from Shrewsbury Prison to lend a hand on the Montgomery canal. The aim is for inmates to learn new skills as they help upgrade sections of the 35-mile waterway. British Waterways regeneration manager Andrew Stumpf said [...] "A lot of prisoners have skills already. If they are not skilled, they can train on the job. There's a wide range of tasks that can be undertaken. Even if people have very few skills, you can match the jobs to everyone's ability so that they can all succeed."'

STRATFORD CANAL

The historical importance of the restoration of the southern section of the Stratford-upon-Avon Canal can only now be fully appreciated, as it stood as a fine example of what could be done. Following its opening in 1964, it gave inspiration and creditability to the many canal restoration projects that followed it. An important feature of that restoration was that much of the labour was voluntary, while offenders from various prisons were brought in to help. At first, some were not particularly enthusiastic, but as time passed, they came to appreciate and later enjoy the work that they were put to. Some prisoners arrived at the worksite with the intention of doing as little as possible, and obtaining the maximum benefits from their time outside the walls, and many tools were 'lost'. In only one case did the prison officer on charge of a working party manage to hang on to all the tools, and he was an ex-regimental sergeant major who tolerated no messing about, insisting on a tool check each night and morning. Nevertheless, by the time prison work parties had been operating for some time, most of the men were not only working hard – initially they wanted a soft option – but were taking pride in their achievements; so much so, that the original volunteers started to vet the long waiting list of inmates trying to get onto the scheme. The key to success was always the use of adequate and experienced supervisors.

In the 1950s, there was still the occasional bit of commercial carrying on some of Britain's canal system, but this was not the case on the southern section of the Stratford, where the canal had been pretty much left to itself since the 1930s. And then in January 1956, following an appeal in the Inland Waterways Association Bulletin, a meeting took place at New Street Station, Birmingham. A start was made on true restoration in March 1961; the manager was David Hutchings, who gave up his career as an architect for the project. The book *Save the Stratford Canal* by Guy Johnson does not relate how Hutchings came to get permission to use prisoners along with other volunteers, but get it he did, and the report states,

The new top gate of Lock 31 (Bishopton) has been installed, as have the paddle starts and paddles. The lock walls, overflow weir etc. are now being demolished and rebuilt by prisoners from Winson Green Gaol. The condition of the walls of this lock is more serious than any we have yet encountered. It will be necessary to entirely demolish, for its full length and height, the offside wall together with the down stream approach wall: large areas of the towing path side wall and approach wall will also have to be demolished and rebuilt.

Lapworth, the start of the southern section of the Stratford-upon-Avon Canal.

Certainly, the repairs to that lock were only a tiny fraction of the whole restoration, but one can achieve a sense of the work involved. Work went on with more voluntary labour coming from the Staffordshire & Worcestershire Canal Society while six 'star' prisoners from the same Birmingham gaol arrived to work for eight hours a day, six days a week. To transport their 'star' workers, an old van was bought, while the prison commission extended the scheme after initial problems had been overcome. A later report read,

> LABOUR – we are very fortunate indeed to have been able to obtain labour from the Prison Commission. Without this help, which at present comprises an average of a dozen prisoners each day, there would be little hope of completing the programme on time. It is hoped that the size of the parties from Winson Green Gaol will be increased, and a single-decker ex-London bus has now been bought to transport extra prisoners between the prison and the gaol.

One of the big jobs on the restoration was the work of digging out and repairing the Bancroft Basin, where the Stratford Canal terminated and met the River Avon. This work was also undertaken by prisoners, but not, this time, only from Birmingham; other goals were willing to try the scheme, and now Winson Green inmates were being joined by their 'associates' from Maidstone. They began on 14 October 1963, joined by the Royal Engineers, who thoughtfully brought along their own drag-lines to dredge the basin. An estimated 10,000 tons of mud was removed, loaded into tipper lorries loaned from Messrs John Laing, and driven away by prisoners – their privileges and responsibilities were growing. It's just sad that the Stratford Council was not as cooperative with this project as the prison services, who proved to be capable of more. For, in the following year, a design for a replacement footbridge was agreed between the National Trust and the council, which was then constructed by prisoners at Wormwood Scrubs.

Bancroft Basin, Stratford, where prisoners put in so much effort.

BRINDLEY PLACE, BIRMINGHAM:
A MODEL FOR CANAL AND CITY REGENERATION

Brindley Place in Birmingham is a fine example of mixed use, where good design and the adoption of key principles result in the creation of a safe, accessible and attractive environment. The old hidden world of Birmingham's canals of the nineteenth and twentieth centuries received a complete transformation of image, impressing visitors and locals alike. A newspaper report stated, 'A courageous city council, along with highly skilled architects, and the developers Argent, created a bright, new, mixed-use urban neighbourhood. And it is fervently hoped that this careful balance of leisure, retail, business and residential property will provide an enjoyable and sustainable environment. London has had its own flagship development schemes, but Brindley place provides valuable lessons for other cities and towns, with water frontage, wishing to emulate its grand success.'

Maybe some of you who have slightly longer memories, and lived near to Birmingham, recall a centre stifled by an inner ring road, loads of ghastly concrete, and a dirty decayed canal environment, set in high canyons of disused and gloomy brickwork. Much of that has now gone – though not all was bad – while we now benefit from a vision that has created attractive, spacious pedestrian areas, set on a variety of levels, with sculptures and other eye-pleasing architectural features and buildings. But there is no doubt that a vision was required for that transformation, and much credit goes to Birmingham City Council for assisting in that highly imaginative strategy.

Approach to Birmingham with the National Indoor Arena to the left.

Brindley Place, Birmingham.

In October 1995, the canalside development won a top international honour award. The 'Excellence on the Waterfront' award was given to the City of Birmingham for the regeneration project at 'The Water's Edge', and Birmingham was the first British city to be presented with this award. A newspaper said, 'Landlocked Birmingham has shared the top honours with Boston and New York, in an international competition to find the world's best waterfronts.' The city scooped the honour for the regeneration of the 200-year-old canal side around Gas St Basin and Brindley Place. It includes 1,000 yards of waterfront with offices, restaurants, bars and shops. Nevertheless, crime has not gone far, for less then a mile away, there is still drug-taking, mugging and the occasional rape of a homosexual rent boy – another modern crime. Yes, crime has not been eradicated, just relocated.

So, although figures are not specifically available for the waterways, it has been noted that only 15 per cent of criminal acts are pre-planned, with the remaining 85 per cent being opportunistic. The nature of criminal activity can be placed in two categories, namely crime against property, which includes antisocial behaviour, vandalism/wilful damage, graffiti, arson, theft, burglary and illegal tipping, which is a more organised form of littering and is also annoying, and then there are the crimes against the person, which includes mugging, assault, rape, indecent exposure, threatening behaviour and, of course, the very occasional murder.

Attacks on boats and their crews appears to be increasing, whether the boat is moving or not. Terry Darlington for instance, the well-known travel writer, sadly had his boat burnt out in November 2009, while others nearby were sunk. Surely this was no accident, and all waterways users need to be vigilant without being a vigilante. Terry remarked that although his boat had braved the English Channel, and been through some difficult adventures, he had lost his boat at a supposedly secure home mooring. Boat burnings and sinkings are, of course, very worrying, but there are many kinds of crimes. Some may argue that placing wooden bollards at locks is a crime and waste of money, especially when BW have so many other important things to spend their money on. Many boaters would agree that licence evasion needs to be tackled. In a recent (2010) magazine, BW stated that licence evasion dropped again in 2009 – almost halving since 2007. Only 5.3 per cent of boats observed in November 2009 were not displaying a valid licence, compared to 10.4 per cent in 2007. In the same report, it said that the biggest improvement was in the former South East region, which included the southern Grand Union, where evasion had been historically high. Unfortunately, there had been a small increase in the South West, including the Kennet & Avon (had they moved?). Simon Salem, BW's marketing Director, said that the fall was a result of enforcement work, the new £150 charge for late payment, and the 'License it or Lose it Campaign' by which seventy boats were seized in 2009 alone. Boats worth less than £1,000 were generally crushed, while more valuable ones were sold.

Publications to inform boaters have included *Keep Your Boat Secure* (HMSO); *Keep Your Boat Crimetight* (Home Office and Central Office of Information); *Safe Mooring or Thieves' Paradise?* (British Marine Industries Federation); *Waterways Design Manual*, Volume 1, Buildings and Facilities; Volume 2, 3, etc.; *Waterside Design and Planning Handbook* (British Waterways, 1998); *Defensible Space, People and Design in the Violent City* (Oscar Newman, Jan 1972); *Vandalism* (edited by Colin Ward, 1973); *Canalside Development in Birmingham, Design Guidelines Consultation Copy* (Birmingham City Council Planning and Architecture).

WATERWAY CRIMES IN FILM AND LITERATURE

Rivers and canals have often featured in film and literature. We started this book by looking at an excerpt from one of Charles Dickens' novels where he describes conditions inside Newgate gaol, but Dickens is only one of many writers who have placed their dramas right next to the waterways of Britain. The list includes *The Full Monty*, *28 Weeks Later*, various episodes of *EastEnders*, *Inspector Morse*, *Boon*, *Coronation Street*, *Taggart*, which used the Forth & Clyde Canal as a backdrop, *Midsomer Murders* and James Bond, *The World is Not Enough*, to name a few. BW's spokesman Richard Millar stated, 'If you only see Scotland's canals on screen, you might be forgiven for thinking that the waterways are usually the setting for crime-solving or the home of mysterious monsters. Certainly, it has not passed the criminal mind that the often-lonely canals and rivers are a great place to dump anything from a shopping trolley to a corpse.

Certainly, the internet is a useful tool for research, but you can't always trust what you find there. For instance, on BW's website, Waterscape, it was reported that the crime-fighting duo of Dalziel and Pascoe – why are there always two of them? –were looking for clues along the Birmingham & Fazeley Canal at Edgbaston. Anyone who knows their canals is well aware that it is the Birmingham & Worcester Canal that goes through Edgbaston; so they are obviously looking in the wrong place. BBC producers have filmed many scenes for the soap EastEnders on London's canals, but by far the most famous was 'Dirty' Den's apparent death in 1989 and then subsequent return in 2003, filmed in Alperton on the Grand Union Canal, which was watched by over 16 million viewers.

Colin Dexter – writer of Inspector Morse – was obviously fascinated by the Christina Collins case when he came across it, because he based his story *The Wench is Dead* upon its framework, though he did, of course, set the whole thing on the Oxford canal. In Dexter's plot, he has Morse (1989) lying in a hospital bed recovering from a bleeding ulcer. To fill his time, Morse comes across an historical murder – now moved to 1859, of a woman found in the canal. Morse is so convinced that the two men hanged for the crime were innocent, he sets out to prove it from his sick bed – one hundred years later. In series seven of *Midsomer Murders* ('The Green Man'), the detective Troy wins promotion to inspector, but before he can decide on his future, a local canal tunnel collapses while undergoing restoration, revealing ancient human bones with a recent skeleton hidden among them. As Chief Inspector Barnaby investigates this suspicious death, Troy is sent to the woods near Midsomer Worthy, where a wild man, called Tom, has been attacked by a group of youths. Then one of the teenagers is caught in a mantrap and shot dead. Immediate suspicions fall on Tom. Many of the scenes were shot in Hertfordshire. In a later episode entitled 'Dead in the Water', a body is found in the River Thames during the annual Midsomer Regatta: ladies' man Guy Sweetman appears to have been killed after arguing with his friends Philip Trent and John Parkway from the rowing club.

C. S. Forester (1899-1966) was also a prolific writer of novels that included *The Gun* and the *African Queen*, a fabulous story featuring Humphrey Bogart, set on a river. But in recent years, his most popular creation has been his maritime hero Horatio Hornblower, as a result of the television series in which Ioan Gruffudd played the lead role and Robert Lindsay was Sir Edward Pellew. Hornblower became the umbrella title of a series of television drama programmes based on a Royal Naval officer during the French Revolutionary Wars and the Napoleonic Wars. The series was produced by the British broadcaster Meridian Television and shown on ITV in 2008. Of course, most of the action is seen from the fighting deck of a ship of the line of the Napoleonic era, but in one story, not yet filmed (*Hornblower and the Atropos*), Hornblower takes a trip on a narrow boat with his wife and child across country. The first chapter, devoted to this canal trip, commences,

> Having climbed up through the locks, the canal boat was now winding over the pleasant Cotswold country. Hornblower was bubbling with good spirits on his way to take up a new command, seeing new sights, travelling in an entirely new way, at a moment when the entirely unpredictable English weather had decided to stage a clear sunny day in the middle of December.

Hornblower was making this fictitious journey along the Thames & Severn Canal from Gloucester to London because it was almost as quick as, and infinitely cheaper than, the stagecoaches – here we have similarities with Christina Collins' decision. Forester then goes on to describe their journey:

> There were two tow lines attached to timber heads; one boatman rode as postillion on the rear horse, controlling the lead horse with shouts and the cracking of his whip. In the stern sat the other boatman, surly and with one hand missing and replaced by a hook; with the other he held the tiller and steered the boat round the curves with a skill that Hornblower admired.

The journey continues through a lock and a view of a grey stone lock house before horses are changed. And then, as they approach a tunnel along a deep cutting, the horses go wild and the drunken postillion is severely injured. Of course, Hornblower – ever the hero – then steps in to assist the one-handed captain to leg through the tunnel (Sapperton) and saves the day. Thus Forester writes a first-class account of a canal trip, but he does make the point that one of the two tow ropes were attached to the stern, which is something I have never come across – so maybe even the best of novelists get the technical details wrong from time to time.

We have mentioned Charles Dickens a few times in this volume, and indeed many of the stories in this book are truly from Dickens era. He occasionally set his scenes by water, but none more so than in the novel *Our Mutual Friend*, filmed by the BBC in 2001, starring Keeley Hawes, Anna Friel, Paul McGann, David Morrissey and Timothy Spall. As always, Dickens unleashes a motley set of characters – one could say creatures – living mainly on the banks of the filthy Thames, where Lizzie Hexam and her father make a sort of living in part by retrieving dead bodies from the water.

The essential plot concerns a John Harmon who is set to inherit a fortune on the understanding that he marries pretty but poor Bella Wilfur, who he has never met. Harmon is cast into the river at the beginning of the story and decides to 'play Dead'. His plan is to pretend to be an ordinary chap so that he can find out if Bella will marry him for love and not for his money.

As a side plot, the very poor but very pretty Lizzie Hexam attracts the interests of two very different men. One is the brooding and mean-tempered Mr Headstone, a local schoolmaster who has dragged himself up by education, and the born into money but lazy Eugene Wrayburn. Lizzie in desperation runs away to a small village – very close to a waterway accessed by a narrow lock. Wrayburn, much in love, and desirous of finding a sort of salvation from that love, tracks her down. Unfortunately, the spurned Headstone follows him and tries to drown him in a pool, only to be saved by Lizzie herself.

Unfortunately for Bradley Headstone, his attempt to kill Wrayburn was secretly observed by the crafty lockkeeper Rogue Riderhood, who then sets out to blackmail Headstone. An interesting scene for canal lovers then opens up in which Headstone grabs Riderhood and both fall and drown in the icy lock. I watched the lock scenes several times but could not identify the location. The lock came immediately from a junction with a canal or river; had a very attractive lock house, and there was a range of hills in the distance. So, maybe it was filmed on the Cotswolds canals (which I am not familiar with), but then again, the whole scene could just as easily be an invention of the filmmaker's art.

Staying for a moment with the River Thames and associated waterways, one could not find a more contrasting scene from the Dickens one just mentioned than with the 2000 version of the James Bond movie *The World Is Not Enough*, featuring Pierce Brosnan as the famous spy. I shall not attempt to explain the plot but simply focus on the high-speed water chase on the Thames in London. Here, the outdoor footage was shot on the River Thames eastwards towards the Millennium Dome. The canal footage of the chase where Bond soaks the parking wardens was filmed at Wapping, and the boat stunts in Millwall Dock and under Glengall Bridge were filmed at the Isle of Dogs. Would Dickens have loved it? Impossible to say, but I am sure that he would have loved writing for television.

MORE CRIME TODAY?

A question often asked is: is there more crime today than in the past? Incumbent governments will always argue, and indeed present seemingly honest statistics, that they are doing a fine job when it comes to tackling crime. It is always the job of the opposition to prove otherwise, and they will throw a second contradictory set of numbers at us, and the water's muddy. We now see that tackling crime has great political overtones. Some commentators have concluded that successive governments of all hues are not really interested in cutting crime, because cutting crime costs money. Still, they like to present the image that they are. In 1997, for instance, Tony Blair repeated the phrase that if he and his government were voted into power they would be 'Tough on crime and Tough on the causes of crime'. It was a good slogan, but a recent report in a daily newspaper stated that some violent crimes had risen by as much as 40 per cent since Labour came to power. So, let us look at some simple figures.

In 1921, there were 103,000 reported crimes for a population of 37,886,689, or in other words, one reported crime for every 367 people. Forty years later, that ratio was one reported crime for every fifty-six people – a huge rise in reported crimes; but by 2001, the ratio was one in 10.2. I think those figures say it all, so that nowadays we talk about the fear of crime – because that's how many folk feel.

Of course, you may be interested in your own experiences with crime, knowing full well that it is inadvisable to moor your boat in some areas, or go for a walk – especially if you are a female along certain urban towpaths. Taking myself as an example, I can state that in a five-year period, I was burgled once and had my car vandalised twice – of course, this was not on the waterways, but it is still general crime.

In Dickens' day, as we have seen, criminals may have been treated too harshly; for instance, transportation for the theft of a few items of clothes appears very draconian. Just imagine if we applied that kind of punishment today: why, a large proportion of teenagers and adults would be herding sheep in Australia. But then again, many would conclude that the pendulum has swung too far the other way and that the law has 'gone soft'. Sensible folk believe that the only way to seriously deter criminal activity is to introduce much stiffer penalties. Nevertheless, the government, police and the judiciary seem much against it. A recent news report said, 'DON'T PUT BURGLARS IN JAIL, COURTS TOLD', and went on to say, 'Burglars should not be jailed unless they cause damage or hurt someone, government advisors said yesterday.' (March 2010) The sentence advisory panel called for judges and magistrates not to hand down prison sentences to 'ordinary' burglars who were responsible for minimal loss or damage – So its ok to steal then – just don't hurt anybody? This seems a very poor policy when one considers that police recorded more than 284,000 burglaries in 2009, a 1 per cent increase over 2008.

The liberal elite and left wing governments have long viewed crime to be caused by poverty or other social ills, and treated the criminal as though he is a victim with his own social and psychological problems. Therefore, millions have been spent on a whole raft of benefits to raise the standard of living, ignoring (or worse, hiding) the fact that crime has and is escalating. People are materially far better off then they were in Dickens day but are blatantly more dishonest.

In the book *A Brief History of Crime*, Peter Hitchens points out that 'the most serious mistake made by modern democracies is to go soft on criminals'. And to underscore that, in a TV interview, one high-ranking police officer said that dealing with crime should be everyone's responsibly. Of course, it's wonderful when the ordinary person on the street can give helpful information to the police, but tackling and preventing crime is the job of the police force – that's what we pay them for.

The average citizen is very much aware, from several well-reported incidents, that it is usually complete folly to tackle criminals on their own for two good reasons. Firstly, that he or she may then be targeted by the same criminals, or just as bad, targeted by the police. Yes, your law-abiding person is often in a lose-lose situation. But can't criminals be reformed you ask?

Many books and papers have been written about the possibility of transforming the criminal into a law-abiding person, and it is a most laudable endeavour. And yes, a small percentage do go through such a transformation, maybe following a religious conversion or the sudden realisation that crime does not pay; but this is the minority.

I quote from another headline, which stated, 'THE SORRY TRUTH IS MANY SEX OFFENDERS CAN'T BE REHABILITATED.' The author of that statement, Dr Ludwig Lowenstein, one of Britain's leading experts on paedophiles, went on to say, 'The British judicial system invests tremendous faith in the rehabilitation of criminals. A key principle of the modern approach to crime is that offenders should not just be punished but should also be reformed – so that they are equipped to participate in society again, and no longer represent a danger to the public.'

But that belief has taken a severe knock in recent days with the continuing story of Jon Venables, killer of James Bulger, who is back in prison after breaching the terms of his release – 2001. There is no doubt that this young man received extensive support throughout the eight years he served in a young offender's institution, including intensive therapy and education. But it hasn't worked. This case demonstrates s harsh truth that society must face up to: some paedophiles and sex offenders (and probably many other criminals) are set upon a life course of crime and are beyond rehabilitation.

What your average law-abiding citizen wants is a government, police force and judiciary that will seriously deal with criminality of all sorts and provide a punishment that *may* just alter the criminal's mind – if not, at least lock him away for a very long time in a prison that punishes and does not supply drugs, so that the rest of us can live in peace. So, I am sorry if I leave this book on somewhat of a sour note, but this is the real situation, and if there is not a radical overhaul of the way that the government, police and judiciary view and tackle crime and criminals, it will only increase.

Also Available from Amberley Publishing

George and Robert Stephenson: The Railway Revolution
L. T. C. Rolt

ISBN: 978 1 84868 164 4
£14.99

Available from all good bookshops or order direct
from our website www.amberleybooks.com

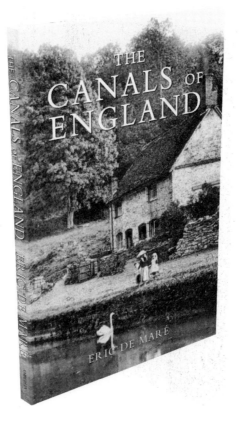

Also Available from Amberley Publishing

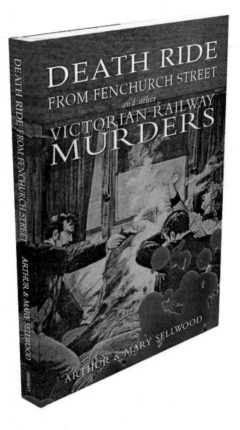

*Death Ride from Fenchurch Street
and other Victorian Railway Murders*
Arthur *&* Mary Sellwood

ISBN: 978 1 84868 495 9
£12.99

Available from all good bookshops or order direct
from our website www.amberleybooks.com